DOUG FIELDS
& MATT McGILL

\\\ BASED ON THE BOOK BY WHITNEY T. KUNIHOLM + SCRIPTURE UNION

Copyright ©2014 Whitney T. Kuniholm

All Rights Reserved. Except as permitted under the U.S. Copyright Act of 1976, no part of this publication may be reproduced, distributed, or transmitted in any form or by any means, or stored in a database or retrieval system, without prior written permission of the publisher.

Published by CrossSection
940 Calle Negocio #175
San Clemente, CA 92673
800-946-5983
crosssection.com

Scripture Taken from the Holy Bible, New International Version®, NIV®. Copyright © 1973, 1978, 1984, 2011 by Biblica, Inc.™

Book + Jacket design by Crosssection

Set in Gotham & Scala

First Edition: August 2014

Printed in the USA

ISBN 978-0-9899537-5-7

THIS BOOK IS DEDICATED TO ALL THE AMAZING YOUTH WORKERS WHO SPEND THEIR TIME AND ENERGY HELPING POINT TEENAGERS TO JESUS. THANK YOU FOR YOUR COMMITMENT TO YOUNG LIVES, DISCIPLESHIP, AND LIVING OUT YOUR FAITH IN FRONT OF A YOUNG AND IMPRESSIONABLE AUDIENCE. YOU ARE OUR HEROES.

—DOUG FIELDS & MATT MCGILL

CONTENTS

Start Here: Read This First 8

OLD TESTAMENT

In the Beginning 17
① ② ③ ④ ⑤

Abraham, Isaac, Jacob 25
⑥ ⑦ ⑧ ⑨ ⑩

The Story of Joseph 33
⑪ ⑫ ⑬ ⑭ ⑮

Moses & the Exodus 41
⑯ ⑰ ⑱ ⑲ ⑳

The Law & the Land 49
㉑ ㉒ ㉓ ㉔ ㉕

The Judges 57
㉖ ㉗ ㉘ ㉙ ㉚

The Rise of Israel 65
㉛ ㉜ ㉝ ㉞ ㉟

The Fall of Israel 73
㊱ ㊲ ㊳ ㊴ ㊵

The Psalms and Proverbs 81
㊶ ㊷ ㊸ ㊹ ㊺

The Prophets 89
㊻ ㊼ ㊽ ㊾ ㊿

NEW TESTAMENT

The Living Word ········· 99
(51) (52) (53) (54) (55)

The Teachings of Jesus ········· 107
(56) (57) (58) (59) (60)

The Miracles of Jesus ········· 115
(61) (62) (63) (64) (65)

The Cross ········· 123
(66) (67) (68) (69) (70)

The Church Is Born ········· 131
(71) (72) (73) (74) (75)

The Travels of Paul ········· 139
(76) (77) (78) (79) (80)

Paul's Letters to the Churches ········· 147
(81) (82) (83) (84) (85)

Paul's Letters to the Leaders ········· 155
(86) (87) (88) (89) (90)

The Apostles' Teaching ········· 163
(91) (92) (93) (94) (95)

Revelation ········· 171
(96) (97) (98) (99) (100)

Author Bios ········· 179

START HERE

READ THIS FIRST

WHAT THIS IS GOING TO DO FOR YOU!

We are so excited for the journey you're about to take. Whether it was your idea to pick up this book or you were encouraged by a parent or friend, it's a good choice! Way to go! Actually, it's a courageous choice to spend time reading and thinking about and discussing God's Word. It could be the choice that changes your life! Congratulations!

In the following pages you'll be invited into God's incredible story. It's our prayer that somewhere in his story you'll find out where your own story intersects.

From the beginning of the Old Testament to the end of the New Testament you'll discover God's amazing love revealed through an incredible plan. It's a wild journey and we are inviting you to join us.

Whether you are new to the Bible or you've been reading it for years, you're about to discover 100 reading selections that will give you a great overview of the Bible's central storyline.

WHAT'S THE DEAL WITH THE ESSENTIAL 100?

These Essential 100 readings contain a carefully selected list of short Bible passages that will expose you to God's story through the historical books, poetry and wisdom, the prophets, the Gospels, Acts, the Epistles, and Revelation. If you don't currently know what those are... you will! There are 50 Old Testament passages and 50 passages from the New Testament and each one is specifically chosen to help you better understand God, his ways, and his plans for you.

So, why did we chose 100—and not 30 or 50 or even 10? Fair question. We believe this number creates an opportunity for you to dig deeper into God's Word and at the same time helps you develop a Bible reading habit that will benefit you for the rest of your life. There are no "rules" in how long it will take... Just keep reading until you finish the 100, and then you can celebrate your big accomplishment.

TAKE THE ESSENTIAL 100 CHALLENGE

We're calling this the "Essential 100 Challenge" as a way to help you, your youth ministry, your friends, your family, and even your entire church read through the 100 Scriptures together.

Join the challenge! You can do it. Actually, if the people in your church aren't part of the challenge, step up and challenge them to join too. What you're holding is the youth edition of *The Essential 100 Study Guide*, but there's also another version for the non-youth in your church that can be found at ScriptureUnionResources.com.

HOW TO GET THE MOST OUT OF THIS BOOK

Please know that there's no ONE WAY to use this book and begin your journey to cover the big picture of the Bible. You have the freedom to do whatever you want... you choose the time and the schedule. Do whatever works best for you. Nothing is dated so you can use it at any time of the year and you can read it in 100 days—or 1000 days. Again, it's flexible and it's all up to you. Here are some specific tips to help you get the most out of your time:

1. Each reading is flexible enough for you to spend a minimal amount of time with the daily reading or an hour or so digging-in and making this a more profound experience. You can go deeper by answering the questions and really thinking through the passage so that you can discover how it relates to your life. You control the amount of time you want to spend with each reading.

2. Before you read, select a place that's comfortable for you where you won't be easily distracted. In today's world, it is so easy to get sidetracked! If reading at the same time each day is helpful for developing a habit, go that route.

3. Be sure to pick up a copy of *The Essential 100 Bible Reading Planner*, our popular punch-out card that helps you track your 100-day reading progress. It's a lot of fun to use and you can order them from ScriptureUnionResources.com. We also encourage you to use the check circles in the table of contents to help you track your reading.

4. Try to find at least one other person to take The Essential 100 Challenge with you (parent, friend, youth pastor). Our experience is that you're more willing to keep going when you know you're not on the journey alone.

5. For each reading, we encourage you to follow our simple guided structure: (1) Pray it, (2) Read it, (3) Think about it, (4) Try it, (5) Write it, and (6) Meditate. Once you learn these simple actions, you can use them anytime you read a Bible passage. Here's how it works:

- **PRAY IT:** Before you read, ask God to help you understand his Word. We've written out a sample prayer to get you started.

- **READ IT:** Read the Bible passage slowly and thoughtfully. If you have time, read it more than once (or even aloud)... make the time to "take it in."

- **THINK ABOUT IT:** We provide a basic question to get you thinking about what you just read. You can answer it in your mind, talk about it with a friend, or write your response in the space provided.

- **TRY IT:** We want you to learn from God's Word and then do something connected to what you just read. Many followers of Jesus... Uh, well, they don't follow. They read, puff up with knowledge, and stay comfortable. We want you to put your faith into action in very real ways. Knowledge that travels from your head to your heart will impact your day-to-day life. If you don't like our "try it" suggestions, that's okay, just try something else.

- **WRITE IT:** There's something powerful that can happen when you put your thoughts, ideas, questions, dreams, and prayers down on paper. We're big fans of journaling and want to challenge you to write stuff down. So grab a notebook or journal and keep it nearby.

- **MEDITATE:** Meditate is a fancy word for "reflect" or "ponder." The idea here is to take one Scripture and think about it a little more. If you have extra time, write the verse down somewhere and take it with you throughout the day.

6. Finally, discuss what you read. Talk over the readings with a friend, your family, or within your small group. Adding dialogue to your study will transform your devotion time into a powerful spiritual experience. At the end of every 5 readings, we've given you some questions to get your discussion started. Again, you don't have to use our questions if you have better ones that will create more significant dialogue.

GROUP DISCUSSION INSTRUCTIONS

When you gather, use your first meeting to answer some basic questions: who will lead or facilitate discussion, and what's the best time/place/frequency of your meetings? Get those answers and you're on your way!

When you meet, keep in mind these following principles:

- **BE PREPARED:** Encourage every member to read the passages for the week prior to the meeting.

- **ENCOURAGE DISCUSSION:** Consider allowing everyone to share one thing he/she learned from the reading. Use the questions we've provided as a starting point for the group discussion. Don't feel pressure to answer all the questions! We've given you several to choose from and your small group time may not be enough to get through them all. No big deal! Encourage the group members to take some time to answer the other questions on their own. As you are sharing your thoughts, make it clear that everyone should have an opportunity to participate and be careful not to allow one person to dominate the conversation.

- **LEARN AND LIVE:** Share examples of how you've tried to live out what you've learned. That's when the Bible will really come alive to you and others in your group.

START HERE

DON'T RACE THROUGH THIS BOOK; WORK THROUGH IT SLOWLY.

We encourage you not to speed through these readings so you can say, "I finished!" Our goal is that you'll gain more knowledge and love for God and his Word. As you read through these essential 100 passages you'll be able to discover for yourself why God loves you deeply and wants to guide your life.

Our prayer for you is that over the next few months, the Bible's greatest story of God's love will come alive for you as never before. Please don't allow these 100 readings to be the end of your journey in the Bible. Let it become the beginning of a lifetime adventure of connecting with Jesus through the Bible, prayer, and discussion.

If you would like another resource like this one, you might consider *The Essential Jesus* (100 Essential readings from the Old and New Testament that draw you closer to Jesus) and you can get that at ScriptureUnionResources.com.

We're excited to hear about your spiritual growth!
Doug Fields, Matt McGill, and Whitney T. Kuniholm

www.DougFields.com
www.DownloadYouthMinistry.com
www.ScriptureUnion.org

THE ESSENTIAL 100 YOUTH EDITION

OLD TESTAMENT

OVERVIEW

IN THE BEGINNING

In these readings, we discover some important truths about God, the world, and people.

God is the creator of the universe and everything in it. No one and no thing is "above" God or greater than him. Creation was perfect, without sin (disobedience and separation from God). It wasn't long before sin entered the world through Adam and Eve. After generations of wicked disobedience, God flooded the earth to wipe out all life—except for Noah, his family, and enough animals to repopulate the planet. Not long after the flood, the effects of sin were again evident. In their pride, people came together to build a tower to reach up to heaven. God destroyed the tower and confused their language so they couldn't work together.

God created us to be dependent on him, not independent from him.

These passages explore the following important questions:

- How did everything begin?

- Do I have a purpose?

- What are the effects of disobedience to God?

- Why do I need God?

1 IN THE BEGINNING... THE VERY BEGINNING...

PRAY IT:
God, thank You for creating me, the world, and the universe. You are greater than I can imagine. Help me to know You better.

READ IT:
Genesis 1–2

THINK ABOUT IT:
God created everything: you, the world, even that annoying person in your 3rd period class. God created love and joy and fun. What does this say about God? What kind of power does he have?

TRY IT:
Three times today, make the effort to notice something beautiful and give thanks to God.

WRITE IT:
Before you finish, take a little time to write your thoughts, questions, concerns, and/or prayers here...

....

....

....

....

MEDITATE:

ROMANS 1:20
For since the creation of the world God's invisible qualities—his eternal power and divine nature—have been clearly seen, being understood from what has been made, so that people are without excuse.

2 TROUBLE IN PARADISE

PRAY IT:
God, I love You even when I have to think about difficult truths. Help me to hear Your voice today.

READ IT:
Genesis 3

THINK ABOUT IT:
When you hear the word "sin," what comes to mind? Why do you think we can't even measure up to our own ideas of what it means to be perfect?

TRY IT:
Work to be extra aware of your temptations today. When you are faced with a decision to do something wrong, ask God for help. Ask a friend for prayer too!

WRITE IT:
Before you finish, take a little time to write your thoughts, questions, concerns, and/or prayers here...

MEDITATE:

JAMES 1:13-15
When tempted, no one should say, "God is tempting me." For God cannot be tempted by evil, nor does he tempt anyone; but each person is tempted when they are dragged away by their own evil desire and enticed. Then, after desire has conceived, it gives birth to sin; and sin, when it is full-grown, gives birth to death.

3 THE PURGE

PRAY IT:
Lord, teach me to understand Your ways, and help me to accept the consequences for my actions.

READ IT:
Genesis 6:5–7:24

THINK ABOUT IT:
How does the world today compare with that in Noah's time? When was the last time you experienced a painful consequence that was the direct result of your action? What did you learn?

TRY IT:
What is one new way you can be a good example of what it means to love God and follow Jesus?

WRITE IT:
Before you finish, take a little time to write your thoughts, questions, concerns, and/or prayers here...

MEDITATE:

PSALM 29:11
The Lord gives strength to his people;
the Lord blesses his people with peace.

4) GOD MAKES A PROMISE

PRAY IT:
Father, thank You for Your promises, which You always keep. I find strength in Your trustworthiness.

READ IT:
Genesis 8:1–9:17

THINK ABOUT IT:
Trust is the foundation for any significant relationship. God always keeps his promises, but it's still difficult to trust him. What is one area in your life where you can trust God more?

TRY IT:
Write down one promise from God to you and put it in a place where you will read it every day for the next week.

WRITE IT:
Before you finish, take a little time to write your thoughts, questions, concerns, and/or prayers here...

....

....

....

....

MEDITATE:

PSALM 119:50
My comfort in my suffering is this:
Your promise preserves my life.

5 THE TOWER OF BABEL

PRAY IT:
Father, thank You for being bigger than my understanding. Help me to know You more, and forgive me when I try to limit or control You.

READ IT:
Genesis 11:1-9

THINK ABOUT IT:
The Tower of Babel was built out of pride. The people had a desire to be equal to or better than God. Another way to describe pride is self-sufficiency. When/where are the times in your life when you feel that you don't need God because you can handle everything on your own?

TRY IT:
Find a small rock and write the word "pride" on it. Put it in a place where you'll see it regularly and be reminded not to build your own personal "Tower of Babel."

WRITE IT:
Before you finish, take a little time to write your thoughts, questions, concerns, and/or prayers here…

MEDITATE:

JAMES 4:10
Humble yourselves before the Lord, and he will lift you up.

GROUP DISCUSSION QUESTIONS:

IN THE BEGINNING

Purpose: To understand basic truths about God, humankind, and sin.

GENESIS 1-2
1. Based on these passages, what do you think God is like?
2. We were created in the image of God. What do you think that means?
3. Do you think God loves you and that you are important to him? Why or why not?

GENESIS 3
4. Write a definition of sin. What do you think most people believe about sin?
5. Why do you think sin was so attractive to Adam and Eve?

GENESIS 6:5-7:24
6. Do you ever find yourself in a situation like Noah, when God asked you to do something big for him?
7. What makes you feel guilty? How do you handle those feelings?

GENESIS 8:1-9:17
8. Have you ever experienced forgiveness from someone close to you?
9. Have you ever experienced God's forgiveness? Share what you learned from these experiences.

GENESIS 11:1-9
10. The motivation for building the Tower of Babel was pride. When might pride be a sin? When might it be a good thing?
11. Do you think it is always dangerous to want to "make a name" for yourself as the people in Babel did? Why or why not?

BEFORE THE NEXT TIME:
Read again and reflect on Genesis 1:26. Thank God that you have been made in his image and think about what difference that makes (or should make) in how you see yourself and others.

OVERVIEW

THE ESSENTIAL 100 YOUTH EDITION

ABRAHAM, ISAAC, JACOB

Long ago, God worked powerfully in the lives of three people: Abraham, Isaac, and Jacob.

God spoke to Abram and challenged him to leave his country. Abram had faith and obeyed. God promised Abram that he would become the father of many nations—not just one nation, but many! Abram and his wife Sarai grew old and still had no children, so they took matters into their own hands. Sarai told Abram to have a child with her maid-servant, and he did. In spite of this, God was still faithful. God reaffirmed his promise to Abram and changed his name to Abraham. Sarai's name was changed to Sarah. In their old age, Abraham and Sarah gave birth to Isaac.

Sometime later, when Isaac was a young boy, God commanded Abraham to sacrifice Isaac. As a man of faith, Abraham obeyed. Imagine how difficult it must have been to give up his son, whom he had waited so long to have with Sarah! In the final moments, God told him to stop and provided a ram for the sacrifice.

Isaac had two sons, Jacob and Esau. They were opposites in every way and competed against one another. This led to conflict and division. Later in their lives, they "buried the hatchet" and restored their relationship. In this section, we'll explore the stories of a dysfunctional family that God used for his great purposes.

God called Abraham to a higher purpose and established his family with many blessings.

These passages explore the following important questions:

- Does God call people to serve his purpose?

- Can I trust God's promises?

- How can I restore broken relationships in my life?

6 GOD CALLS ABRAM

PRAY IT:
Dear God, thank You for calling me to You to experience Your love and enjoy a close relationship with You.

READ IT:
Genesis 12

THINK ABOUT IT:
God called Abram to something radical: to leave his people, his homeland, to follow him. What is God's call in your life? Chances are, he's not calling you to leave your homeland, but what changes do you need to make to follow him faithfully?

TRY IT:
God promised Abram land for his descendants. What is one promise that God has made to you?

WRITE IT:
Before you finish, take a little time to write your thoughts, questions, concerns, and/or prayers here...

MEDITATE:

ROMANS 4:3
What does Scripture say? "Abraham believed God, and it was credited to him as righteousness."

7) GOD'S PROMISE TO ABRAHAM

PRAY IT:
Father, thank You for Your promises. Help me to trust them more than the things of this world.

READ IT:
Genesis 15

THINK ABOUT IT:
Abraham and Sarah were childless, even into their old age. It must have been extremely difficult to trust in God's promise to make Abraham a father of nations. God's way is often more difficult than our own way, but we can trust him to always provide what we need.

TRY IT:
What are the two biggest barriers in your life that are keeping you from trusting God?

WRITE IT:
Before you finish, take a little time to write your thoughts, questions, concerns, and/or prayers here...

MEDITATE:

GALATIANS 3:7
Understand, then, that those who have faith are children of Abraham.

8 GOD PROVIDES

PRAY IT:
Dear God, You are the provider of everything I need. Help me to trust in You more than the things of this world.

READ IT:
Genesis 21:1–22:19

THINK ABOUT IT:
God wants to be the number one priority in your life, even more important than the gifts he gives you. It is silly for a child to love Christmas presents more than their parents, yet this is what we sometimes do with God. The Giver is greater than the gifts!

TRY IT:
Make a list of at least three things God has blessed you with and give him thanks. If those gifts were gone, would you still praise God?

WRITE IT:
Before you finish, take a little time to write your thoughts, questions, concerns, and/or prayers here...

MEDITATE:

MATTHEW 6:33
But seek first his kingdom and his righteousness, and all these things will be given to you as well.

9 JACOB & ESAU COMPETE

PRAY IT:
Dear Lord, even though my family isn't perfect, I thank you for the people who care for me.

READ IT:
Genesis 27–28

THINK ABOUT IT:
All sorts of things can tear a family a part. For Isaac, his son Jacob was greedy, and he wanted his older brother's (Esau) inheritance. Jacob took advantage of his dying father to gain what rightfully belonged to his brother.

TRY IT:
How has your family made you into the person you are today? What are five or six qualities of a healthy family? What can you do today to help build these qualities in your family?

WRITE IT:
Before you finish, take a little time to write your thoughts, questions, concerns, and/or prayers here...

MEDITATE:

PHILIPPIANS 2:3-4
Do nothing out of selfish ambition or vain conceit. Rather, in humility value others above yourselves, not looking to your own interests but each of you to the interests of the others.

10 JACOB & ESAU RESTORE THEIR RELATIONSHIP

PRAY IT:
My Father in heaven, give me the humility to restore the broken relationships in my life.

READ IT:
Genesis 32–33

THINK ABOUT IT:
Jacob and Esau were able to restore their broken relationship. Based on your reading, what are some important action steps a person can take to fix a broken relationship?

TRY IT:
Think about a broken relationship in your life—family or friend—and take at least one step towards restoring or improving that connection. We were made for meaningful relationships!

WRITE IT:
Before you finish, take a little time to write your thoughts, questions, concerns, and/or prayers here...

MEDITATE:

ROMANS 12:8
... if it is to encourage, then give encouragement; if it is giving, then give generously; if it is to lead, do it diligently; if it is to show mercy, do it cheerfully.

GROUP DISCUSSION QUESTIONS:

ABRAHAM, ISAAC, JACOB

Purpose: To learn about God's call and test of Abraham and how healthy families operate.

GENESIS 12

1. What do you think it means to be called to something?
2. God called Abraham to leave his relatives and country and go to a new place. Do you think God still calls people today? If so, how? To what?
3. Do you have a calling in life? If so, how would you describe it?

GENESIS 15

4. Abraham was called to be a father of many nations, but without children, this calling seemed impossible. What are some "impossible" situations you are facing right now? How could faith make the difference for you?

GENESIS 21:1-22:19

5. Being called to sacrifice his son was a real test for Abraham. Describe how God has tested you in the past.
6. How might a time of testing make one a better person? Has it done that for you? If so, how?

GENESIS 27-28

7. Jacob and Esau didn't have a healthy family. In your opinion, what are the characteristics of a healthy family?
8. In what ways has your family shaped you, for good or bad?

GENESIS 32-33

9. Jacob and Esau weren't close. In fact, Jacob thought they were enemies. Have you ever had a strained or broken relationship with a close friend or family member? If so, how did you deal with it?
10. From your experience, how can broken family relationships be healed? How could Jacob and Esau's relationship have been healed quicker?

BEFORE THE NEXT TIME:

As you reflect on the promises God made to Abraham and how God fulfilled them, ask God to show you something of the plans and promises he has for you.

OVERVIEW

THE STORY OF JOSEPH

Joseph, the 11th son of Jacob, was his father's favorite son. As you can imagine, this created tension with his eleven other brothers. As a young man, Joseph had a dream: one day he would rule over his entire family. When he told his dream to his brothers, they got so angry that they decided to sell him into slavery in Egypt. While he was a slave, he was falsely imprisoned. Through it all, Joseph continued to be faithful to God.

God gave Joseph the ability to interpret dreams. When the Pharaoh had a dream that no one could interpret, he called on Joseph. The meaning was clear: Egypt would experience seven years of plenty followed by seven years of famine. Pharaoh put Joseph in charge of the entire country, to prepare everyone for the years of famine. What a story of riches to rags to even greater riches!

When famine hit the land, Jacob's family was forced to come buy food from Egypt. After some struggle, Joseph was reconciled and reunited with his family. Joseph knew and declared to his brothers that, though they had intended to harm him, God used that situation to work out his saving purposes for Joseph's family, God's people Israel, and even the Egyptians.

God is in control, even when our lives look and feel like they are out of control.

These passages explore the following important questions:

- Is God really in control?

- How do I respond when people treat me badly?

- What does family reconciliation look like?

11 JOSEPH SOLD INTO SLAVERY

PRAY IT:
God, I'm thankful for my family. Please strengthen our relationships and show me how to love them more.

READ IT:
Genesis 37

THINK ABOUT IT:
What were some of the biggest problems in Joseph's family? How do you typically handle problems or conflicts in your family?

TRY IT:
Take some time to make a list of ten great things you see or would like to see in your family. Ask God to show you your part in making those a reality for your family.

WRITE IT:
Before you finish, take a little time to write your thoughts, questions, concerns, and/or prayers here...

MEDITATE:

ROMANS 8:28
And we know that in all things God works for the good of those who love him, who have been called according to his purpose.

12 FROM RAGS TO RICHES

PRAY IT:
God, help me to trust in You when I face problems in my life. Give me the strength and wisdom I need to get through the hard times.

READ IT:
Genesis 39–41

THINK ABOUT IT:
Joseph faced incredible trials: he was sold into slavery by his brothers, thrown into prison unfairly, and lived most his life away from his family and homeland. God often uses difficult times to make us more like Jesus. What was Joseph's attitude toward his problems?

TRY IT:
Think about the last two difficulties you faced. How did you respond in each situation? What could be a response next time?

WRITE IT:
Before you finish, take a little time to write your thoughts, questions, concerns, and/or prayers here...

....

....

....

MEDITATE:

PSALM 20:7
Some trust in chariots and some in horses, but we trust in the name of the Lord our God.

13 JOSEPH ABUSES HIS POWER

PRAY IT:
Lord, thank You for loving me. Give me the strength to be self-controlled when I have the chance to get back at others.

READ IT:
Genesis 42

THINK ABOUT IT:
Joseph was harsh in dealing with his brothers. He used deception, falsely accused them, and abused his power to get what he wanted. Do you think he had a "right" to get revenge? Why or why not?

TRY IT:
When was the last time you gave in to the temptation to retaliate and get even with someone who hurt you? If possible, make things right by apologizing to that person some time this week.

WRITE IT:
Before you finish, take a little time to write your thoughts, questions, concerns, and/or prayers here...

MEDITATE:

LEVITICUS 19:16
Do not go about spreading slander among your people. Do not do anything that endangers your neighbor's life. I am the Lord.

14 JOSEPH ACHIEVES HIS GOAL

PRAY IT:
Dear God, help me to want what You know I need. Thank You for loving me even when I chase after the wrong things.

READ IT:
Genesis 43–44

THINK ABOUT IT:
Joseph wanted to see his brother Benjamin, and he used any means necessary to achieve his goal. After he got what he wanted, he still wasn't happy, so he continued down the path of treating his brothers harshly. Why do you think he continued rather than change?

TRY IT:
Trusting God to provide is better than turning to selfish ways to get what we want. What is one thing in your life that you need to trust God to provide?

WRITE IT:
Before you finish, take a little time to write your thoughts, questions, concerns, and/or prayers here…

....

....

....

MEDITATE:

PROVERBS 10:18
Whoever conceals hatred with lying lips and spreads slander is a fool.

15 JOSEPH FINALLY COMES CLEAN

PRAY IT:
Father, help me to be honest and tell the truth, even when it's difficult.

READ IT:
Genesis 45:1–46:7

THINK ABOUT IT:
In this memorable passage, Joseph finally tells the truth and experiences some powerful emotions. What do you think Joseph was feeling? Why was telling the truth so powerful?

TRY IT:
The more we lie, the easier it gets, and soon it becomes a regular habit. Is there an area in your life where deception has become acceptable (e.g., cheating at school, telling "white lies," over-exaggerating)? What do you need to come clean?

WRITE IT:
Before you finish, take a little time to write your thoughts, questions, concerns, and/or prayers here...

MEDITATE:

EPHESIANS 4:25
Therefore each of you must put off falsehood and speak truthfully to your neighbor, for we are all members of one body.

GROUP DISCUSSION QUESTIONS:

THE STORY OF JOSEPH

Purpose: To learn lessons from Joseph's story about unfair treatment, family conflicts, and how to deal constructively with them.

GENESIS 37

1. Like most families, Joseph's family experienced conflict and tension. What causes tension and conflict in your family?
2. In your opinion, what is the best way to resolve family conflict?

GENESIS 39-41

3. Joseph wasn't treated fairly: his brothers sold him into slavery and his master had him falsely imprisoned. What's the toughest situation you've experienced?
4. What did you learn through that tough situation?

GENESIS 42

5. When his brothers came to him in Egypt, Joseph pretended not to know them. Why do you think people sometimes hide their true feelings?
6. Have you ever been in a situation where you felt it necessary to hide your true feelings? If so, tell why and what happened.
7. In what kinds of situations do you feel comfortable sharing the "real you"?

GENESIS 43-44

8. Joseph had a plan to see if his brothers—who'd hurt him so badly in the past—had changed. How have you found healing from the unresolved hurts from the past?
9. How could you help others who are struggling with past hurts? What can you share from your own experience?

GENESIS 45:1-46:7

10. What are some of your most important experiences from the past that have shaped who you are today? Did they have a positive or negative impact?
11. Joseph formed a regular pattern of deceiving his brothers, but eventually he spoke the truth. What would help you become more truthful, even avoiding "little" lies?

BEFORE THE NEXT TIME:

If this study has raised any personal issues in your life and family relationships that you still struggle with, talk these over with God this week and ask for help to resolve them. Don't hesitate to talk with a friend you respect or an adult leader at church.

OVERVIEW

MOSES & THE EXODUS

Moses was one of the greatest and most significant Old Testament figures. Moses grew up as a privileged member of Pharaoh's royal family. At the age of 20, he had to flee Egypt when he murdered an Egyptian who had been abusing one of the Israelites. Years later, the Lord appeared to him in a burning bush and called him to go to Egypt and tell Pharaoh to "let my people go" free from their slavery. After 10 miraculous plagues against Egypt, the Pharaoh lets the people go—only to hunt them down soon after they leave. Stuck between an impossible sea and an angry army, God pushes back the sea and the Israelites pass on dry ground. The army takes the same "path" and ends up being swallowed by the waters.

Our God saves: the Lord rescued his people from slavery in Egypt and destruction in the desert.

These passages explore the following important questions:

- What does it look like to hear God speak?

- Can God use me even though I have limitations and weaknesses?

- Does God have the power to care for my needs and overcome the problems I'm facing?

16 THE BIRTH OF MOSES

PRAY IT:
Dear God, thank You for Your protection in my life. Help me to understand today's reading so I can hear You speak to me.

READ IT:
Exodus 1–2

THINK ABOUT IT:
God protected Moses, literally keeping him from being killed at birth. How has God protected and cared for you? Why do you think God protects us?

TRY IT:
Start a list in your journal of all the ways that God protects, cares, provides, and prepares you for the work to which he is calling you.

WRITE IT:
Before you finish, take a little time to write your thoughts, questions, concerns, and/or prayers here...

MEDITATE:

PSALM 32:7
You are my hiding place;
you will protect me from trouble
and surround me with songs of deliverance.

17 THE BURNING BUSH

PRAY IT:
Lord, I want to see You more clearly. Help me to follow You more nearly.

READ IT:
Exodus 3:1–4:17

THINK ABOUT IT:
God used a burning bush to get Moses' attention. How does God usually get your attention? What are the most significant ways you meet with God?

TRY IT:
God gave Moses a huge challenge—to free the people of Israel from slavery in Egypt. What dreams has God given you? If you knew God would be with you every step of the way, what could you do for God?

WRITE IT:
Before you finish, take a little time to write your thoughts, questions, concerns, and/or prayers here...

MEDITATE:

HEBREWS 11:23
By faith Moses' parents hid him for three months after he was born, because they saw he was no ordinary child, and they were not afraid of the king's edict.

18 THE TEN PLAGUES ON EGYPT

PRAY IT:
Dear Lord, thank You for loving me. Sometimes it can be hard to understand Your ways. Help me to follow You today.

READ IT:
Exodus 6:28–11:10

THINK ABOUT IT:
The Lord judged Egypt because the Pharaoh wouldn't obey God and let the Israelites go to worship him. Often, our poor decisions and disobedience bring bad consequences into our lives.

TRY IT:
Are there any problems in your life that you are blaming on others even though it was your fault? What would it look like for you to shift your perspective?

WRITE IT:
Before you finish, take a little time to write your thoughts, questions, concerns, and/or prayers here...

MEDITATE:

HEBREWS 4:13
Nothing in all creation is hidden from God's sight. Everything is uncovered and laid bare before the eyes of him to whom we must give account.

19 THE PASSOVER

PRAY IT:
Lord, my life is a journey with You. Thank You for loving and providing for me.

READ IT:
Exodus 12:1-42

THINK ABOUT IT:
The Passover is a big-time event in the Bible. Not only was it celebrated every year by the Israelites, but Jesus redefined this celebration on the night before he died on the cross.

TRY IT:
There can be no doubt: the Passover was intense. God took the life of every firstborn son in Egypt. God also sent his Son, Jesus, to die on the cross for the sins of the world. Take a moment today and write out a prayer of thanks to God for his grace in your life.

WRITE IT:
Before you finish, take a little time to write your thoughts, questions, concerns, and/or prayers here...

....

....

....

MEDITATE:

PSALM 9:1
I will give thanks to you, Lord, with all my heart;
I will tell of all your wonderful deeds.

20 CROSSING THE RED SEA

PRAY IT:
Father, help me to trust You with every part of my life, even in the darkest moments.

READ IT:
Exodus 13:17–14:31

THINK ABOUT IT:
The Israelites were stuck: their backs were up against a wall (an impassable sea) while facing an unbeatable army. In the moment, it didn't seem like they had any options. When was the last time you felt utterly stuck?

TRY IT:
Have you had any moments in your life when you had to totally rely on God? How can you build your trust in God so that the next time you are in a situation that seems hopeless, you can have faith that God will act?

WRITE IT:
Before you finish, take a little time to write your thoughts, questions, concerns, and/or prayers here...

....

....

....

MEDITATE:

PROVERBS 3:5-6
Trust in the Lord with all your heart and lean not on your own understanding; in all your ways submit to him, and he will make your paths straight.

GROUP DISCUSSION GUIDE:

MOSES & THE EXODUS

Purpose: To learn from the way Moses encounters God and from the way God's actions in the special times of our lives shape and define us.

EXODUS 1-2
1. Moses' mother had to trust God to protect her son. What is something you need to trust God with?
2. From growing up in Pharaoh's household and living among the royalty of Egypt, Moses faced both opportunities and difficulties. As you look at your life, what opportunities and difficulties have you encountered?

EXODUS 3:1-4:17
3. Moses encountered God at the burning bush. What are some ways that people encounter God today? How do you encounter him? What is the most powerful way you've encountered God?
4. Have you, like Moses, ever felt inadequate and unprepared for something God wanted you to do? What happened?

EXODUS 6:28-11:10
5. God is always working "behind the scenes," and it seems like we only notice some of what he's doing. When you take a moment to think about it, where do you think God is working in the world around you?
6. What would it look like for you to be more open and aware of what God is doing?

EXODUS 12:1-42
7. What does Passover show you about God's character? What questions does it force you to ask?
8. Does God's judgment on the Egyptians seem fair to you? Why or why not?

EXODUS 13:17-14:31
9. The Exodus was a defining moment for the Israelites. What have been the defining moments in your life? How did they affect you?
10. Have you ever ignored God when you knew the right thing to do? What led you to act this way? What were the results?

BEFORE THE NEXT TIME:
Reflect on Moses' interactions with God and the way God personally delivered his people from slavery. Consider all the miraculous signs and how God fulfilled his promises. How does this change the way you see or interact with God? Thank the Lord, the great I AM who fulfills his promises.

OVERVIEW

THE LAW & THE LAND

21-25

God continued to be with his people after their trek through the Red Sea. He lead them to Mount Sinai, and they camped there for about ten months. God spoke to Moses and gave him the Law (which includes the Ten Commandments). The purpose of the Law was to teach the people how to worship God and set them apart from the other nations. The people disobeyed God and were condemned to wander the desert for forty years. After the wanderings, Joshua led Israel into the Promised Land.

God is trustworthy. He fulfilled all of his promises to Abraham.

These passages explore the following important questions:

- What kind of life honors God?

- What does it mean to worship?

- Will God be with me when he calls me to big things?

21 THE TEN COMMANDMENTS

PRAY IT:
Lord, thank You for giving us Your wisdom for living a meaningful life. Help me to better understand Your will for my life.

READ IT:
Exodus 19:1–20:21

THINK ABOUT IT:
Some people consider the Ten Commandments outdated. What do you think? What use could they have in our modern society? In your opinion, which commands are most needed?

TRY IT:
Re-read the Ten Commandments. Which one do you have the most difficulty keeping? Write that one out on a note card and put it in a place where you will read it every day this week.

WRITE IT:
Before you finish, take a little time to write your thoughts, questions, concerns, and/or prayers here...

MEDITATE:

EXODUS 20:1-3
And God spoke all these words: "I am the Lord your God, who brought you out of Egypt, out of the land of slavery. You shall have no other gods before me."

22 FALSE WORSHIP

PRAY IT:

Father, forgive me for the times when I let other things become more important than You.

READ IT:

Exodus 32–34

THINK ABOUT IT:

At first, it may seem crazy that the Israelites were so quick to worship false gods. However, this gives us insight about the human heart. We easily forget the great things that God does for us and quickly look to other places for comfort, joy, significance, etc.

TRY IT:

Worship is a human activity, because everyone worships something. Our highest priority is what we worship. What are some of the "false gods" that you see in our society? What are some of the things that people idolize and worship?

WRITE IT:

Before you finish, take a little time to write your thoughts, questions, concerns, and/or prayers here...

MEDITATE:

PSALM 135:13-18

Your name, Lord, endures forever, your renown, Lord, through all generations. For the Lord will vindicate his people and have compassion on his servants. The idols of the nations are silver and gold, made by human hands. They have mouths, but cannot speak, eyes, but cannot see. They have ears, but cannot hear, nor is there breath in their mouths. Those who make them will be like them, and so will all who trust in them.

23 ISRAEL'S NEW LEADER

PRAY IT:
My God, thank You for Your constant presence in my life. No matter what the day brings, I know You are my strength.

READ IT:
Joshua 1

THINK ABOUT IT:
Joshua had some big shoes to fill: Moses was one of the greatest of Israel's leaders. What was God's command to Joshua? Why do you think he needed to hear that from God?

TRY IT:
It's difficult to live a bold and courageous life. What are some things or situations in your life that tend to undermine your confidence? What could it look like if God was with you in those moments?

WRITE IT:
Before you finish, take a little time to write your thoughts, questions, concerns, and/or prayers here...

MEDITATE:

PSALM 71:5-8
For you have been my hope, Sovereign Lord, my confidence since my youth. From birth I have relied on you; you brought me forth from my mother's womb. I will ever praise you. I have become a sign to many; you are my strong refuge. My mouth is filled with your praise, declaring your splendor all day long.

24 ISRAEL CROSSES THE JORDAN

PRAY IT:

Lord, thank You for the times You display Your faithfulness. Help me to trust You more and remember Your blessings.

READ IT:

Joshua 3-4

THINK ABOUT IT:

God stopped a huge river so Israel could cross over into the promised land. He did this to demonstrate his faithfulness and to establish Joshua as their leader.

TRY IT:

The leaders of Israel made a pile of stones as a monument so future generations would know about God's faithfulness. How has God been faithful in your life? Make a list in your journal, and be as specific as you can.

WRITE IT:

Before you finish, take a little time to write your thoughts, questions, concerns, and/or prayers here...

MEDITATE:

PSALM 77:11-12

I will remember the deeds of the Lord;
yes, I will remember your miracles of long ago.
I will consider all your works
and meditate on all your mighty deeds.

25 THE FALL OF JERICHO

PRAY IT:
Powerful God, I trust Your strength more than my own.

READ IT:
Joshua 5:13–6:27

THINK ABOUT IT:
Have you ever felt like God asked you to do something that felt impossible? What happened? How did it make it an impact in your faith?

TRY IT:
Write out Joshua 1:9 on a note card and read it every morning for the next week. Put it in a place where you won't miss it.

WRITE IT:
Before you finish, take a little time to write your thoughts, questions, concerns, and/or prayers here...

MEDITATE:

EPHESIANS 3:20-21
Now to him who is able to do immeasurably more than all we ask or imagine, according to his power that is at work within us, to him be glory in the church and in Christ Jesus throughout all generations, for ever and ever! Amen.

THE LAW & THE LAND

GROUP DISCUSSION QUESTIONS:

THE LAW & THE LAND

Purpose: To see how God wants his people to live and act as those called to be holy and live in close relationship with him.

EXODUS 19:1-20:21

1. Re-read the Ten Commandments. The first four commandments are about our "vertical" relationship with God, and the final six govern our "horizontal" relationships with others. In your opinion, what's the connection between our vertical relationship and our horizontal relationships?
2. Which of the Ten Commandments is most challenging to you and why?

EXODUS 32-34

3. What do you think motivated the Israelites to worship the Golden Calf instead of God, especially after God had done so many great things to save them? What motivates people to worship "things" rather than God today?
4. What situations tend to pull you away from God? Can you do anything to avoid them? If not, how can you still stay strong in your faith when you face temptation?

JOSHUA 1

5. Moses was Joshua's mentor. What qualities make a person a good mentor for others?
6. Do you have a mentor or small group leader? If so, how has he/she helped you in the past? If not, what could you do to find one?

JOSHUA 3-4

7. Take a moment to think about God's promises for your future. What are they? How do they help you make it through the tough times?
8. After the Israelites crossed the Jordan, they set up a pile of stones in order to remember God's faithfulness. What is something great that God has done for you, and what can you do to make sure you never forget it?

JOSHUA 5:13-6:27

9. God told Israel to march around Jericho for a week, and on the last day the walls fell, enabling the army to capture the city. Why do you think God gave them victory in this way?

BEFORE THE NEXT TIME:

Read again Exodus 20:1-17 and read Joshua 1:8. How can you make God's Word and God's law more completely a part of your everyday life?

OVERVIEW

THE JUDGES

During this period of history, Israel wasn't a unified nation, not as we are likely to assume. Israel was a loose association of tribes, united by common ancestry (Abraham, Isaac, and Jacob) and the worship of the same God. Most of the time, leadership was family based. In times of great need, God raised up special leaders for a specific task, usually to throw off the yoke of oppression from a particular enemy.

This was also a period of unfaithfulness and disobedience. The book of Judges paints a downward spiral: (a) the people would reject God, next (b) God would give them over to the hands of their enemies, then (c) the people would cry for help, (d) God would send a judge to save them, leading them into (e) a period of peace.

Even in the midst of constant rejection, God still loved his people and used his power to save them from their enemies.

These passages explore the following important questions:

- What does God's love for me look like when I fail him?

- How can I restore my relationship with God?

- How will God work through me to help others?

26 ISRAEL'S DISOBEDIENCE

PRAY IT:
God, I'm sorry for the times I go my way rather than Your way. Forgive me and show me how I might serve You today.

READ IT:
Judges 2:6–3:6

THINK ABOUT IT:
The generation of Israelites right after Joshua rebelled against God. How quickly they forgot the great things God had done through Moses and then Joshua. What do you think causes people to forget God's blessings?

TRY IT:
What is one practical way you can stay focused on God and growing in your relationship with him? Tell a trusted friend or leader at church so they can be praying for you.

WRITE IT:
Before you finish, take a little time to write your thoughts, questions, concerns, and/or prayers here...

MEDITATE:

DEUTERONOMY 31:24-29
After Moses finished writing in a book the words of this law from beginning to end, he gave this command to the Levites who carried the ark of the covenant of the Lord: "Take this Book of the Law and place it beside the ark of the covenant of the Lord your God. There it will remain as a witness against you. For I know how rebellious and stiff-necked you are. If you have been rebellious against the Lord while I am still alive and with you, how much more will you rebel after I die! Assemble before me all the elders of your tribes and all your officials, so that I can speak these words in their hearing and call the heavens and the earth to testify against them. For I know that after my death you are sure to become utterly corrupt and to turn from the way I have commanded you. In days to come, disaster will fall on you because you will do evil in the sight of the Lord and arouse his anger by what your hands have made."

THE JUDGES

27 DEBORAH LEADS ISRAEL

PRAY IT:
Father, help me to live out my faith without making excuses. I want to follow You.

READ IT:
Judges 4–5

THINK ABOUT IT:
Deborah was a prophet and had considerable influence in Israel. When she told Barak God's command to attack the enemy, he responded with conditional obedience. He said, "I'll obey IF..." Truth is, God isn't looking for us to hide behind our excuses.

TRY IT:
In your own life, where do you offer God the same kind of conditional obedience? What are the "ifs" you tell God rather than following him fully?

WRITE IT:
Before you finish, take a little time to write your thoughts, questions, concerns, and/or prayers here...

....

....

....

MEDITATE:

DEUTERONOMY 6:5
Love the Lord your God with all your heart and with all your soul and with all your strength.

28 GIDEON DEFEATS THE MIDIANITES

PRAY IT:
Father, thank You that when I am afraid, You provide the assurance I need through the power of Your presence.

READ IT:
Judges 6–7

THINK ABOUT IT:
Gideon felt too weak to accomplish the task God gave him. How did God respond and provide the help that Gideon needed? When God calls us, he also provides the strength to be faithful.

TRY IT:
Think of one scary thing God is calling you to do, but you feel like you aren't good enough. How can you overcome your fear and trust God this week?

WRITE IT:
Before you finish, take a little time to write your thoughts, questions, concerns, and/or prayers here...

MEDITATE:

ISAIAH 43:2
When you pass through the waters, I will be with you; and when you pass through the rivers, they will not sweep over you. When you walk through the fire, you will not be burned; the flames will not set you ablaze.

29 SAMSON DEFEATS THE PHILISTINES

PRAY IT:
Dear Lord, thank You for the gifts You have given me. Forgive me when I get too prideful and trust myself more than I trust You.

READ IT:
Judges 13–16

THINK ABOUT IT:
Samson's pride got him in big trouble. He felt his great strength would stay with him even after he broke his vows to God. Sometimes we believe the lie that we are good enough on our own and that we don't need God.

TRY IT:
Take a few moments and think about your strengths. Are there any situations in your life where you trust more in them rather than God? How does your pride short-circuit your relationships?

WRITE IT:
Before you finish, take a little time to write your thoughts, questions, concerns, and/or prayers here...

....

....

....

MEDITATE:

PROVERBS 16:18
Pride goes before destruction, a haughty spirit before a fall.

30 THE STORY OF RUTH

PRAY IT:
Thank You for loving me, Lord. Help me to love others as a reflection of Your work in my life.

READ IT:
Ruth 1–4

THINK ABOUT IT:
What can you learn from Ruth's story and example to help you in your life this week?

TRY IT:
Think of at least one person whom you know who needs to be loved. Make a list of three practical ways that you can show them value and care for them. Act on at least one of your ideas this week.

WRITE IT:
Before you finish, take a little time to write your thoughts, questions, concerns, and/or prayers here...

MEDITATE:

GALATIANS 6:2
Carry each other's burdens, and in this way you will fulfill the law of Christ.

GROUP DISCUSSION QUESTIONS:

THE JUDGES

Purpose: To learn from both the obedience and disobedience of the judges, and how that affected their relationship with him and others.

JUDGES 2:6–3:6

1. The Israelites were stuck in a downward spiral: rejection of God, oppression from enemies, crying out for help, salvation from God through a judge. After a period of peace, they would reject God once again. In your own life, have you seen repeated patterns of ignoring God? What does that cycle look like?
2. Do you experience ups and downs in your relationship with God? With others? Why?

JUDGES 4–5

3. Barak had an attitude that said, "I'll obey you, God, IF..." Describe a time when you were tempted to put an "if" between you and doing the right thing. How were you able to let go of being conditionally obedient?
4. How can your faith give you more courage and confidence? Explain why you think the way you do.

JUDGES 6–7

5. Do you think Gideon was bold or timid? Wise or foolish? Explain your answer.
6. God was clearly guiding Gideon. How do you think God guides people today? What would it look like to be more receptive to his leading?

JUDGES 13–16

7. In your own words, describe Samson's attitudes and actions related to women. Why do you think he was this way?
8. What does it look like to create healthy relationships with the opposite sex? How does our culture work against healthy relationships?

RUTH 1–4

9. What character traits do you notice in Ruth? Which do you admire most and why?
10. Ruth's commitment to Naomi was extreme: she left her homeland to support her mother-in-law. What is something small you can sacrifice this week to serve someone else?

BEFORE THE NEXT TIME:

Following Jesus will last your lifetime, which means there will be ups and downs. Ask God for help. Lean on his strength, not your own. Trust in his promises, not your power. Seek to live a life of sacrifice to serve others.

OVERVIEW

THE RISE OF ISRAEL

Hannah, a woman known for her faithfulness to God, was unable to have children. She cried out to God for a son, and promised to dedicate him to work in the temple. God blessed her with Samuel. He became the last of Israel's judges and the first of her prophets. Near the end of his leadership, the people rebelled against God and asked for a king. They wanted to be like the other nations. God picked Saul, and the people loved him. In the end, Saul proved unworthy and David became the next king. Under his reign, Israel experienced great prosperity.

God works through ordinary people to accomplish his will on earth.

These passages explore the following important questions:

- Does God want to do great things through my life?

- What does it look like to be a servant of God?

- What happens when I ignore God's design in order to copy the world?

31 SAMUEL LISTENS TO GOD

PRAY IT:
Dear God, thank You that You speak to me. Help me to remove the distractions in my life so that I may hear You.

READ IT:
1 Samuel 1–3

THINK ABOUT IT:
It's amazing that the Creator of the universe wants to speak to each and every one of us. Have you ever felt like God was speaking to you? What did he say? How did you know it was him speaking?

TRY IT:
If you are facing a big-time problem, spend some extra time in prayer today. Express your feelings to God and listen to what he has to say.

WRITE IT:
Before you finish, take a little time to write your thoughts, questions, concerns, and/or prayers here...

MEDITATE:

PSALM 34:17-20
The righteous cry out, and the Lord hears them; he delivers them from all their troubles. The Lord is close to the brokenhearted and saves those who are crushed in spirit. The righteous person may have many troubles, but the Lord delivers him from them all; he protects all his bones, not one of them will be broken.

THE RISE OF ISRAEL

32 KING SAUL

PRAY IT:
God, I pray for the leaders in my world: at school and in the government. Give them the wisdom and grace to lead well.

READ IT:
1 Samuel 8–10

THINK ABOUT IT:
The people of Israel rejected God as their king. They wanted to be like the other nations and have a human king. God's design for our lives is always perfect, always the best option.

TRY IT:
Reflect on your life for the last two weeks. In what ways did you reject God's way for you? What happened, and what were the consequences? What can you do to put things back on track for this week?

WRITE IT:
Before you finish, take a little time to write your thoughts, questions, concerns, and/or prayers here…

MEDITATE:

ISAIAH 31:6
Return, you Israelites, to the One you have so greatly revolted against.

33 DAVID & GOLIATH

PRAY IT:
Lord, help me to confront my challenges today, trusting in Your awesome power.

READ IT:
1 Samuel 16:1–18:16

THINK ABOUT IT:
David defeating Goliath defies all reason. No one would have picked David to win; however, God's power is always greater than our problems.

TRY IT:
David had the courage to face Goliath because he had an unshakeable faith in God. What is the biggest "Goliath" you are facing in your life? Who could you ask to support you as you take on your next Goliath?

WRITE IT:
Before you finish, take a little time to write your thoughts, questions, concerns, and/or prayers here…

....

....

....

....

MEDITATE:

PSALM 118:6-9
The Lord is with me; I will not be afraid.
What can mere mortals do to me?
The Lord is with me; he is my helper.
I look in triumph on my enemies.
It is better to take refuge in the Lord than to trust in humans.
It is better to take refuge in the Lord than to trust in princes.

34 DAVID & SAUL

PRAY IT:
God, help me to have more respect for others, especially for those with whom I have conflict. Strengthen me so that I might show grace when others bother me.

READ IT:
1 Samuel 23:7–24:22

THINK ABOUT IT:
Saul was on the hunt for David, a full-blown vendetta to see David captured. However, when David had the opportunity to attack Saul, he didn't take it. His self-control came from his faith in God.

TRY IT:
Take time today to pray for someone who is difficult for you to get along with. Make an effort to respond to him/her with positivity.

WRITE IT:
Before you finish, take a little time to write your thoughts, questions, concerns, and/or prayers here...

MEDITATE:

ROMANS 12:17
Do not repay anyone evil for evil. Be careful to do what is right in the eyes of everyone.

35 KING DAVID

PRAY IT:
Lord, thank You for having a plan for my life. I know You have made me to do great things in Your Name.

READ IT:
2 Samuel 5–7

THINK ABOUT IT:
David lived an incredible life and did amazing things for God. Rather than take the credit, he was quick to glorify God. He never forgot his humble roots (a shepherd) even though he was king over Israel.

TRY IT:
David excelled at giving thanks to God. Make a list of 20 things you are thankful to God for.

WRITE IT:
Before you finish, take a little time to write your thoughts, questions, concerns, and/or prayers here...

MEDITATE:

1 CORINTHIANS 15:56-58
The sting of death is sin, and the power of sin is the law. But thanks be to God! He gives us the victory through our Lord Jesus Christ. Therefore, my dear brothers and sisters, stand firm. Let nothing move you. Always give yourselves fully to the work of the Lord, because you know that your labor in the Lord is not in vain.

GROUP DISCUSSION QUESTIONS:

THE RISE OF ISRAEL

Purpose: To discover the qualities that God desires in those who lead his people.

1 SAMUEL 1-3

1. Hannah cried out in desperation to God for a son. When was the last time you were desperate? What happened? Do you normally go to God when you are in need? Explain why or why not.
2. God clearly spoke to the boy Samuel, and Eli gave him great wisdom. When you hear God's leading in your life, do you have an attitude that says, "Speak, Lord, your servant is listening"? What keeps you from responding like this?

1 SAMUEL 8-10

3. In your opinion, what character traits make for a good leader?
4. What leaders in your life do you admire and why?

1 SAMUEL 16:1-18:16

5. According to the Bible, what motivated David to challenge Goliath? Has a similar feeling ever driven you? Explain what that was like.
6. Are you—or any of your friends—facing any "Goliaths" in your life right now? What are they and how might faith in God help you confront them?

1 SAMUEL 23:7-24:22

7. In your own words, what was Saul's attitude toward David? Why do you think he felt this way?
8. Is there anyone who has an irrationally negative attitude toward you? How should you respond?

2 SAMUEL 5-7

9. David was a great king! What do you think were his strengths? What were his weaknesses?
10. David was a man of passion. Everything he did for the Lord, he did at 100%. What are some things you are passionate about? What's holding you back?

BEFORE THE NEXT TIME:

Hannah, Eli, Samuel, Saul, David, and Jonathan all can teach us something about living with devotion and integrity before God. They were great leaders of God's people. Reflect on their lives and paint a picture of the kind of leader you know God is calling you to be.

OVERVIEW

THE FALL OF ISRAEL

King David was a man after God's heart and a great king. He also made terrible mistakes: he committed adultery and murder, and he tried to cover it up with lies. His son Solomon was the wisest person who ever lived, yet he also committed severe acts of disobedience. God sent many prophets to warn Israel and her leaders and the message was clear: "Return to God!" In the end, the sins of Israel resulted in a split nation and eventually they were conquered by other nations and sent into exile.

God is merciful, but there are consequences for disobedience.

These passages explore the following important questions:

- Is it possible to resist my temptations?

- What do I need to learn from God about life?

- Am I the kind of person who can listen to things I don't want to hear but need to hear?

36 DAVID & BATHSHEBA

PRAY IT:
God, give me the strength to resist temptations. My desire is to honor You with my life.

READ IT:
2 Samuel 11:1–12:25

THINK ABOUT IT:
David had everything: success, riches, power. All of it was given to him by God. However, even in the midst of plenty, he still wanted more. He was unable to be content with what was his.

TRY IT:
What are the biggest temptations in your life? When is it most difficult for you to be self-controlled? Share these with a trusted friend and ask him/her to support you in prayer.

WRITE IT:
Before you finish, take a little time to write your thoughts, questions, concerns, and/or prayers here...

MEDITATE:

1 CORINTHIANS 10:13
No temptation has overtaken you except what is common to mankind. And God is faithful; he will not let you be tempted beyond what you can bear. But when you are tempted, he will also provide a way out so that you can endure it.

THE FALL OF ISRAEL

37 KING SOLOMON

PRAY IT:
Thank You, God, for Your wisdom. My insight is not enough. I need You to guide my steps every day.

READ IT:
1 Kings 2–3

THINK ABOUT IT:
Solomon was God's chosen leader for Israel, therefore God offered to give him anything he asked for. If you could have anything from God, what would it be? What is your motive behind your request?

TRY IT:
Would you consider yourself to be wise? What would your parents say? What would your friends say about your wisdom? How could you gain more wisdom in your life?

WRITE IT:
Before you finish, take a little time to write your thoughts, questions, concerns, and/or prayers here...

36-40

MEDITATE:

PROVERBS 2:1-6
My son, if you accept my words and store up my commands within you, turning your ear to wisdom and applying your heart to understanding—indeed, if you call out for insight and cry aloud for understanding, and if you look for it as for silver and search for it as for hidden treasure, then you will understand the fear of the Lord and find the knowledge of God. For the Lord gives wisdom; from his mouth come knowledge and understanding.

38 SOLOMON'S TEMPLE

PRAY IT:
Father, thank You that You are always with me, every moment of the day. Help me to remember Your presence in my life.

READ IT:
1 Kings 8:1–9:9

THINK ABOUT IT:
The Temple was a special place where God's glory was present. Even though God's presence is everywhere—all the time—he was in the temple in a special way so that Israel could worship him there.

TRY IT:
Paul tells us that our bodies are temples for the Holy Spirit (1 Corinthians 6:19). What are some practical ways that you can frequently remind yourself to acknowledge God's presence in your life? Make it a goal to say a dozen one-minute prayers throughout the day.

WRITE IT:
Before you finish, take a little time to write your thoughts, questions, concerns, and/or prayers here…

....

....

....

MEDITATE:

JOHN 4:21-24
"Woman," Jesus replied, "believe me, a time is coming when you will worship the Father neither on this mountain nor in Jerusalem. You Samaritans worship what you do not know; we worship what we do know, for salvation is from the Jews. Yet a time is coming and has now come when the true worshipers will worship the Father in the Spirit and in truth, for they are the kind of worshipers the Father seeks. God is spirit, and his worshipers must worship in the Spirit and in truth."

39 ELIJAH & THE FALSE PROPHETS

PRAY IT:
Dear God, thank You for the good people in my life who teach me what it means to follow You.

READ IT:
1 Kings 16:29–19:18

THINK ABOUT IT:
The people of Israel didn't trust God to provide, so they turned to a false god to meet their needs. Have you ever been impatient with God? In what situations do you tend to give up waiting for God to act?

TRY IT:
On a piece of paper, write down the one thing that you really need to trust God to provide. Fold the paper in half, and on the outside write "God is able." Every day this week, put this need before God in prayer.

WRITE IT:
Before you finish, take a little time to write your thoughts, questions, concerns, and/or prayers here...

MEDITATE:

PSALM 9:10
Those who know your name trust in you,
for you, Lord, have never forsaken those who seek you.

40 THE FALL OF JERUSALEM

PRAY IT:
Dear Father, thank You for Your mercy and grace. I know there are many times that I live according to my selfishness. Change my heart to reflect Yours.

READ IT:
2 Kings 25

THINK ABOUT IT:
The fall of Jerusalem was punishment from God for the Israelites' disobedience. After generations of warnings from God, he took them from the promised land for their sin.

TRY IT:
God's love for us means he gives us the capacity to choose him. When we choose against him, eventually there are consequences. Do you have anything in your life that you need to confess to God?

WRITE IT:
Before you finish, take a little time to write your thoughts, questions, concerns, and/or prayers here...

MEDITATE:

1 JOHN 1:9
If we confess our sins, he is faithful and just and will forgive us our sins and purify us from all unrighteousness.

THE FALL OF ISRAEL

GROUP DISCUSSION QUESTIONS:

THE FALL OF ISRAEL

Purpose: To see how the sin of Israel led to their destruction and exile.

2 SAMUEL 11:1-12:25
1. Respond to this statement: "What I do in my personal life is nobody's business but my own."
2. What do you learn about confrontation based on David being confronted by Nathan?

1 KINGS 2-3
3. If God promised to give you anything you wanted, what would you ask for? Be honest!
4. Solomon's wisdom was legendary. How could you build more wisdom into your life? Who is the wisest person you've ever known? Why do you say that?

1 KINGS 8:1-9:9
5. The worship of Solomon and the people in dedicating the temple was lively and heartfelt. What makes worship come alive for you?
6. What kind of attitude should you choose before coming to church to worship? How can you guard against the entitlement that says, "I need to be entertained" or "This better be good"?

1 KINGS 16:29-19:18
7. Elijah was so spiritually dry and discouraged that he asked God to end his life. Have you ever felt great spiritual dryness or discouragement? Explain the situation.
8. When you are in a spiritually dry season, what is your typical response? What gives you a sense of renewal?

2 KINGS 25
9. The capture of Jerusalem and sacking of the Temple was a terrible disaster. Have you experienced any terrible disasters in your life? If so, what did you learn from them?
10. Describe a time when difficulties or challenges grew you closer to God. What did you learn?

BEFORE THE NEXT TIME:
This week, consider the journey of the Israelites, who fell from great prosperity into exile. Sin, that is, disobedience to God, has consequences. How can you make spending time in the Word of God a higher priority?

OVERVIEW

THE PSALMS AND PROVERBS

The book of Psalms is a collection of worship songs. It's unique in the Bible because not only is it God's Word to us, it is also our words to God. Nearly every human emotion is expressed: from the depths of despair to the heights of joy. The Psalms teach us how to authentically worship God with reckless abandon: we don't have to hold anything back! Our God is the one who is worthy of our worship, in good times and bad.

The book of Proverbs is several collections of short sayings. This book is filled with wisdom and practical advice on a wide range of topics. These memorable verses guide a believer to wisdom, good choices, and spiritual discernment.

These passages explore the following important questions:

- What does it mean to worship God?

- Can I share all of my feelings with God?

- How can I make good choices, every day?

41 THE LORD IS MY SHEPHERD

PRAY IT:
Lord, thank You for caring for me, for leading me, and for refreshing my soul when I need it most.

READ IT:
Psalm 23

THINK ABOUT IT:
What do you learn about God from this Psalm? What does it teach about his character? Which verse is most significant for you and why?

TRY IT:
Are you spiritually tired and need to have your soul refreshed? Read this Psalm again. This time make it your prayer to God.

WRITE IT:
Before you finish, take a little time to write your thoughts, questions, concerns, and/or prayers here…

MEDITATE:

JOHN 10:11
I am the good shepherd. The good shepherd lays down his life for the sheep.

42 HAVE MERCY ON ME

PRAY IT:
Lord, prepare my heart to hear what You have to say to me today.

READ IT:
Psalm 51

THINK ABOUT IT:
There's power confessing our sins to God because we are not designed to hold onto our guilt. His forgiveness is free for us, but it cost him his Son, Jesus.

TRY IT:
Take a moment to make a list of your sins. Ask God to show you where you are missing the mark. Confess them: admit your faults and resolve to leave them in the past. Then tear up the paper and throw it away.

WRITE IT:
Before you finish, take a little time to write your thoughts, questions, concerns, and/or prayers here...

_____

_____

_____

_____

MEDITATE:

PSALM 103:11-12
For as high as the heavens are above the earth,
so great is his love for those who fear him;
as far as the east is from the west,
so far has he removed our transgressions from us.

43 PRAISE THE LORD

PRAY IT:
Lord God, You are wonderful beyond words, more powerful than I can imagine, and more loving than I deserve.

READ IT:
Psalm 103

THINK ABOUT IT:
Make a list of 10 things you think are awesome. Everyone can do this because we were created to recognize the good around us. Every person on the planet offers praise, although we often glorify things according to our selfish desires.

TRY IT:
Create your own praise psalm to God. Use today's reading as a model, but personalize it with specific ideas that are meaningful for you.

WRITE IT:
Before you finish, take a little time to write your thoughts, questions, concerns, and/or prayers here...

MEDITATE:

PSALM 28:6
Praise be to the Lord,
for he has heard my cry for mercy.

44 GODLY WISDOM

PRAY IT:
Father, You are the source of all true wisdom. Give me insight so that I might make better decisions and glorify Your Name.

READ IT:
Proverbs 1–4

THINK ABOUT IT:
What is true wisdom? How would you define it? How does a person become wise? Do you feel like you are on the path to becoming more wise?

TRY IT:
God often speaks to us through others. Do you have a wise mentor in your life? If so, what are the qualities you appreciate about him/her? If not, who would make a great mentor?

WRITE IT:
Before you finish, take a little time to write your thoughts, questions, concerns, and/or prayers here...

MEDITATE:

JAMES 1:5
If any of you lacks wisdom, you should ask God, who gives generously to all without finding fault, and it will be given to you.

45 PROVERBS OF SOLOMON

PRAY IT:
God, give me the practical wisdom I need for today.

READ IT:
Proverbs 16–18

THINK ABOUT IT:
Most of us spend our time chasing things that won't last: popularity, having more stuff, influence... Wisdom has more value than even gold and silver (Proverbs 16:16) because it brings us closer to God.

TRY IT:
Pick two or three proverbs from today's reading and write them on a note card to read every day for a week.

WRITE IT:
Before you finish, take a little time to write your thoughts, questions, concerns, and/or prayers here...

....

....

....

....

....

> **MEDITATE:**
>
> **JAMES 3:13-18**
> Who is wise and understanding among you? Let them show it by their good life, by deeds done in the humility that comes from wisdom. But if you harbor bitter envy and selfish ambition in your hearts, do not boast about it or deny the truth. Such "wisdom" does not come down from heaven but is earthly, unspiritual, demonic. For where you have envy and selfish ambition, there you find disorder and every evil practice. But the wisdom that comes from heaven is first of all pure; then peace-loving, considerate, submissive, full of mercy and good fruit, impartial and sincere. Peacemakers who sow in peace reap a harvest of righteousness.

GROUP DISCUSSION QUESTIONS:

THE PSALMS AND PROVERBS

Purpose: To discover more of God's character and the nature of right living as expressed in the praise, worship, laments, and wise sayings of these books.

PSALM 23

1. In Psalm 23, which image do you relate to the most and why?
2. Take a moment to reflect on your relationship with God, using your own imagery. How would you complete this sentence: "The Lord is my..."?

PSALM 51

3. What do you learn from Psalm 51 about confessing your sins? In what ways is this psalm helpful or encouraging to you?
4. Have you ever experienced a deep sense of God's forgiveness? What led you to asking for forgiveness? What were the results in your life?

PSALM 103

5. What things motivated David to praise God in Psalm 103? What most impresses you about the Lord as David describes him?
6. Write your own definition for the word praise. How would you explain it to someone younger than you?
7. What are five things you can praise God for?

PROVERBS 1-4

8. In the Book of Proverbs, a father imparts wisdom to his son. What wisdom did your parents or other significant adults impart to you?
9. What do you think it means to be wise? Is it different from simply being smart or knowledgeable? If so, how?

PROVERBS 16-18

10. Would you say you are wise? Why or why not? What wisdom have you gained from your experiences in life? From your relationship with God?
11. Try writing two or three "proverbs" on your own and share one with the group.

BEFORE THE NEXT TIME:

Make note this week of some of the characteristics of God that are most meaningful to you and take time to praise him for them. As you reflect on the advice given in both books, ask God to help you incorporate specific aspects into your life.

OVERVIEW

THE PROPHETS

God used ordinary people to warn Israel (and other nations) to stop their evil and return to God. Each prophet was called by God to be his voice to their generation. The prophetic writings make up about one third of the Bible—that's a lot! It may be surprising that less than 5% of their words "predicted" the future. The primary role of the prophet was to warn people to return to God.

These passages explore the following important questions:

- What does it mean to return to God?

- How can I hear God when I'm living in disobedience?

- What might God be calling me toward in my life?

46 THE SUFFERING SERVANT

PRAY IT:

Dear Lord, thank You for sending Your Son Jesus to pay the price for my sins so that the world might be saved through faith.

READ IT:

Isaiah 51–53

THINK ABOUT IT:

No matter how difficult and dark your life may get, God's power is enough. Because he loves us, he sent his Son to save us and give us real life.

TRY IT:

Jesus suffered before he died. He was abandoned by his friends, unfairly accused, whipped, and died in agony on the cross. He did all of this because he loved the world. Think on his sacrifice: How can it make you a different person today?

WRITE IT:

Before you finish, take a little time to write your thoughts, questions, concerns, and/or prayers here...

MEDITATE:

2 CORINTHIANS 1:5-7

For just as we share abundantly in the sufferings of Christ, so also our comfort abounds through Christ. If we are distressed, it is for your comfort and salvation; if we are comforted, it is for your comfort, which produces in you patient endurance of the same sufferings we suffer. And our hope for you is firm, because we know that just as you share in our sufferings, so also you share in our comfort.

47 THE PROPHET JEREMIAH

PRAY IT:
Lord, help me learn to hear Your voice through Your Word, and then to obey.

READ IT:
Jeremiah 1:1–3:5

THINK ABOUT IT:
God used the prophets to warn the wayward people to return to him. Their message was never popular and was always difficult to deliver. It takes faithfulness and integrity to speak God's truth to others.

TRY IT:
Has God given you a difficult message that you need to share with someone you know? Write it down and share it with a trusted friend for insight and support. When the time is right, share the truth with grace.

WRITE IT:
Before you finish, take a little time to write your thoughts, questions, concerns, and/or prayers here...

....

....

....

MEDITATE:

1 CORINTHIANS 2:4-5
My message and my preaching were not with wise and persuasive words, but with a demonstration of the Spirit's power, so that your faith might not rest on human wisdom, but on God's power.

48 DANIEL IN THE LION'S DEN

PRAY IT:
God, sometimes it's not easy to do the right thing. Help me when I'm tempted to leave Your path.

READ IT:
Daniel 6

THINK ABOUT IT:
Daniel was a man of faith and he had vicious enemies who were jealous of him. Through their evil schemes, they had Daniel unfairly sentenced to death. In the end, God was faithful and saved Daniel.

TRY IT:
What would it look like for you to stand up for your faith this week? In a world that ignores or denies Jesus, how can you be different? You don't have to be weird or offensive to demonstrate your faith. Just be yourself, but be a person of integrity.

WRITE IT:
Before you finish, take a little time to write your thoughts, questions, concerns, and/or prayers here...

MEDITATE:

1 TIMOTHY 4:12
Don't let anyone look down on you because you are young, but set an example for the believers in speech, in conduct, in love, in faith and in purity.

49 THE PROPHET JONAH

PRAY IT:
Father, help me to hear Your calling in my life; give me the strength to follow You obediently.

READ IT:
Jonah 1–4

THINK ABOUT IT:
Have you ever wanted to run from God? Why did you want to run? What did you end up doing? What did you learn from the experience?

TRY IT:
Think about the people in your life who don't know Jesus. Make a list of at least five and commit to praying for them regularly. When the time is right, speak up and tell them about God's compassion and grace.

WRITE IT:
Before you finish, take a little time to write your thoughts, questions, concerns, and/or prayers here...

....

....

....

....

MEDITATE:

PSALM 86:15
But you, Lord, are a compassionate and gracious God, slow to anger, abounding in love and faithfulness.

50 THE DAY OF JUDGMENT

PRAY IT:
Father, I want to know You more. Draw me closer to You so that I can become more like Jesus.

READ IT:
Malachi 1–4

THINK ABOUT IT:
Worship is important: God wants our whole heart, our full devotion. When we take a casual view towards worship, it dishonors God.

TRY IT:
What is your usual attitude towards worship? A surrendered heart is faithful and expecting. It says, "This will be good." A consumer mentality is demanding and entitled; it says, "This better be good." Which best describes you: surrendered or consumer? Why?

WRITE IT:
Before you finish, take a little time to write your thoughts, questions, concerns, and/or prayers here...

MEDITATE:

ISAIAH 29:13
The Lord says: "These people come near to me with their mouth and honor me with their lips, but their hearts are far from me. Their worship of me is based on merely human rules they have been taught."

GROUP DISCUSSION QUESTIONS:

THE PROPHETS

Purpose: To look at an important Old Testament prophecy of the coming Messiah and to examine the calling, character, and motivation of some of the prophets.

ISAIAH 51-53

1. Read Isaiah 52:13–53:12. How does this passage describe what happened to Jesus hundreds of years later?
2. This passage describes the suffering of the servant in graphic detail. Why did the servant suffer? What clues from the text support your answer?

JEREMIAH 1:1–3:5

3. What excuses did Jeremiah make to God? Why do you think he resisted God's call?
4. Respond to this statement: "God doesn't always call the gifted, but he always gifts the one he calls."
5. Jeremiah was sent to speak God's message to Jerusalem. If God sent you to speak to your community, school, or friends, what do you think he would want you to say?

DANIEL 6

6. Daniel took a great risk to stand up for his faith. Have you ever had to stand up for what you believe, in spite of significant consequences? What happened?
7. Do you think people today should be more "up front" about their faith in Jesus? Why or why not? What keeps you from expressing your faith more?

JONAH 1-4

8. Have you, like Jonah, ever "run away from God" and ignored his call? What happened?
9. Jonah was disappointed in God for his compassion on Nineveh. How has this attitude shown up in your life? If you are really honest, is there anyone who is "too bad" for church or for Jesus? In what ways do you judge others unfairly?

MALACHI 1-4

10. Malachi talks about "the Day of Judgment." What do you believe about judgment? Do we really deserve it? If God is loving, why will he judge us? Explain why you feel the way you do.
11. Ultimately, we are all accountable to God for our beliefs and actions. How is accountability a good thing? Do you have a friend whom you are accountable to? What does that accountability look like?

BEFORE THE NEXT TIME:

Congratulations! You've finished these readings in the Old Testament. That's a big deal! What was the most surprising or encouraging thing you've learned? Who is one person you can share that with this week?

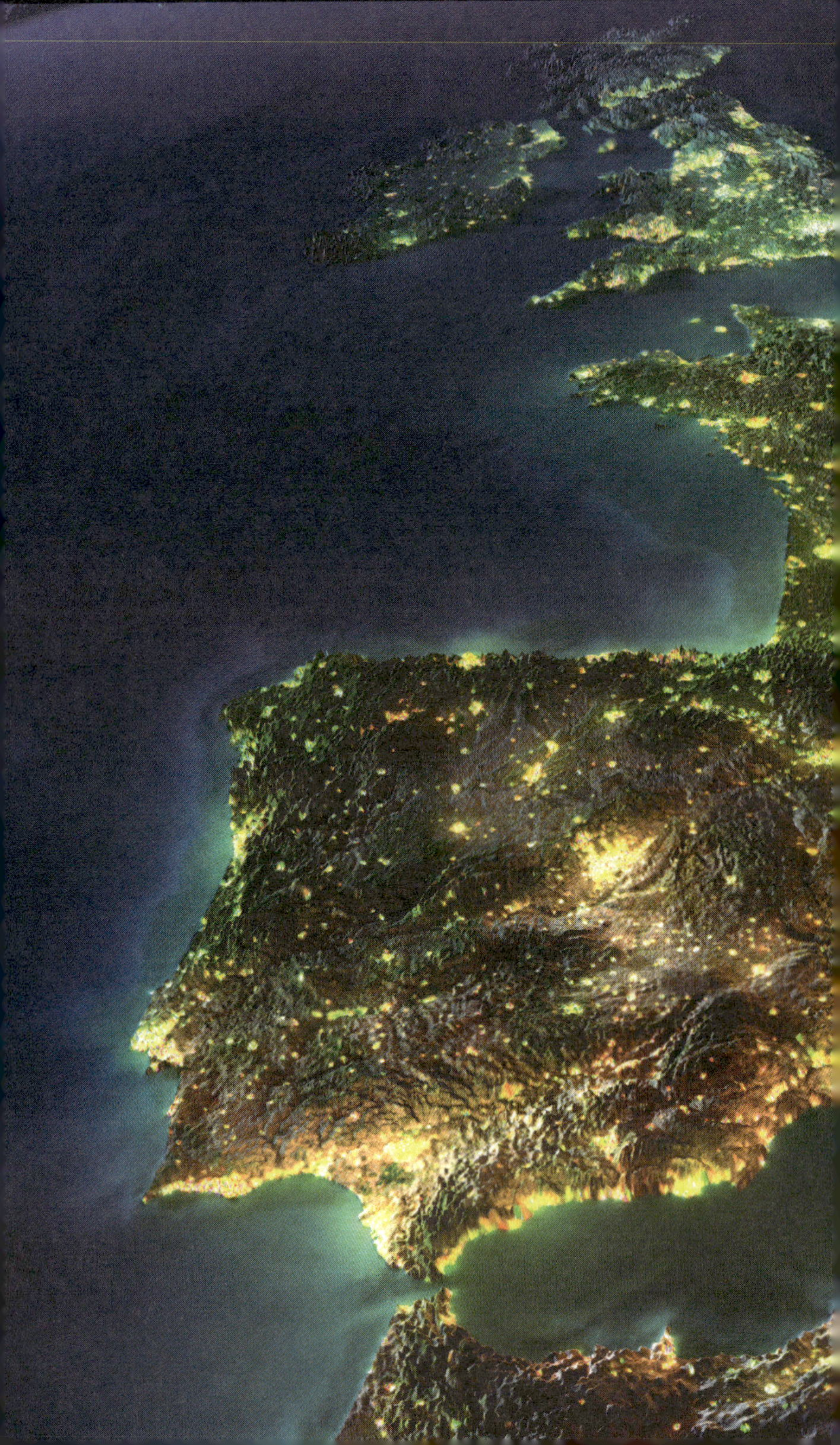

THE ESSENTIAL 100 YOUTH EDITION

NEW TESTAMENT

OVERVIEW

THE LIVING WORD

As you begin your readings in the New Testament, you'll encounter Jesus. He is fully divine and fully human. This mystery defies full understanding. His divinity allowed him to live a perfect life and his humanity made him the perfect sacrifice to pay for our sins. Jesus was tempted by Satan, but did not sin. Since he was a human, Jesus understands our struggles. The Gospels of John and Luke show us how people respond to Jesus: some with outright rejection and others with wholehearted acceptance.

These passages explore the following important questions:

- Who is Jesus?
- Does he understand my temptations?
- Why do people reject Jesus?

51 THE WORD BECAME FLESH

PRAY IT:
God, thank You for sending Your Son into the world to demonstrate Your great love for the lost.

READ IT:
John 1:1-18

THINK ABOUT IT:
As you read this passage, what do you learn about Jesus? Does this change or deepen your faith? If so, how?

TRY IT:
If a friend asked you about Jesus, what would you say? In your own words, write what you believe about Jesus (who he is, why he came to earth, what he's like, etc.).

WRITE IT:
Before you finish, take a little time to write your thoughts, questions, concerns, and/or prayers here...

MEDITATE:

COLOSSIANS 1:15-20

The Son is the image of the invisible God, the firstborn over all creation. For in him all things were created: things in heaven and on earth, visible and invisible, whether thrones or powers or rulers or authorities; all things have been created through him and for him. He is before all things, and in him all things hold together. And he is the head of the body, the church; he is the beginning and the firstborn from among the dead, so that in everything he might have the supremacy. For God was pleased to have all his fullness dwell in him, and through him to reconcile to himself all things, whether things on earth or things in heaven, by making peace through his blood, shed on the cross.

52 GABRIEL'S MESSAGE

PRAY IT:
Father, thank You for Your grace. Forgive my sins and take my guilt.

READ IT:
Luke 1

THINK ABOUT IT:
Why do you think it's important that Luke's Gospel is based off of eyewitness accounts? Is there anything in this chapter that is particularly surprising, inspiring, or confusing?

TRY IT:
When Gabriel spoke to Zechariah, he initially responded with fear. Fear keeps us from living the full life God intends. When do you feel fearful? How do you typically respond? What would it look like for you to trust God with your fears? Is there anything that God has asked you to do that makes you feel fearful?

WRITE IT:
Before you finish, take a little time to write your thoughts, questions, concerns, and/or prayers here...

MEDITATE:

1 JOHN 4:18
There is no fear in love. But perfect love drives out fear, because fear has to do with punishment. The one who fears is not made perfect in love.

53 THE BIRTH OF JESUS

PRAY IT:
God, thank You for sending Your Son. Your love means more to me than anything else.

READ IT:
Luke 2:1-40

THINK ABOUT IT:
Jesus entered into the world with humility. His first bed was an animal food trough. His first visitors were lowly shepherds. He wasn't born in a grand palace and visited by kings from all over the earth, even though certainly he deserved this honor!

TRY IT:
After the shepherds had seen Jesus, they spread the word (see Luke 2:17-18). What are some personal and practical ways you can tell others about Jesus in your life? Make a list of five people who don't know Jesus and begin praying for them daily.

WRITE IT:
Before you finish, take a little time to write your thoughts, questions, concerns, and/or prayers here...

MEDITATE:

PHILIPPIANS 2:5-11
In your relationships with one another, have the same mindset as Christ Jesus: Who, being in very nature God, did not consider equality with God something to be used to his own advantage; rather, he made himself nothing by taking the very nature of a servant, being made in human likeness. And being found in appearance as a man, he humbled himself by becoming obedient to death—even death on a cross! Therefore God exalted him to the highest place and gave him the name that is above every name, that at the name of Jesus every knee should bow, in heaven and on earth and under the earth, and every tongue acknowledge that Jesus Christ is Lord, to the glory of God the Father.

THE LIVING WORD

54 JOHN THE BAPTIST

PRAY IT:
Father, help me to focus on Jesus. Remove the distractions in my life.

READ IT:
Luke 3:1-20

THINK ABOUT IT:
The mission of John the Baptist was to prepare the people of Israel for the ministry of Jesus. After reading this passage, how would you sum up John's message in your own words?

TRY IT:
John called people to repent, which literally means to "turn away." In order to focus more on Jesus, what do you need to turn away from?

WRITE IT:
Before you finish, take a little time to write your thoughts, questions, concerns, and/or prayers here...

MEDITATE:

REVELATION 2:5
Consider how far you have fallen! Repent and do the things you did at first. If you do not repent, I will come to you and remove your lampstand from its place.

55 JESUS BEGINS HIS PUBLIC MINISTRY

PRAY IT:
God, thank You for Your strength. Help me to fight temptation so that I may stay on Your path.

READ IT:
Matthew 4:13–4:17

THINK ABOUT IT:
Satan attacked Jesus with temptation when he was at his weakest: Jesus had been fasting for 40 days! When are you at your weakest and most vulnerable to temptation?

TRY IT:
Scripture is a powerful force against temptation because temptation's power is in lies. God's Word teaches us the truth. Think about the three biggest temptations in your life. What are the lies behind them?

WRITE IT:
Before you finish, take a little time to write your thoughts, questions, concerns, and/or prayers here...

MEDITATE:

1 CORINTHIANS 10:13
No temptation has overtaken you except what is common to mankind. And God is faithful; he will not let you be tempted beyond what you can bear. But when you are tempted, he will also provide a way out so that you can endure it.

GROUP DISCUSSION QUESTIONS:

THE LIVING WORD

Purpose: To learn more about Jesus by exploring the miracle of the incarnation, the humility of his birth, the message of John the Baptist, and his temptation by Satan.

JOHN 1:1-18
1. If someone asked you, "What do you believe about Jesus?" what would you say?
2. Why do you think it's important to know that Jesus created the universe? How could this truth impact the way you live your life?

LUKE 1
3. How would you have felt if you were Elizabeth or Mary, Zechariah or Joseph?
4. Zechariah and Mary were quite surprised (that's an understatement!) by the angel's visit. Has God ever done something surprising in your life? If so, what happened?

LUKE 2:1-40
5. In the devotional, you were challenged to make a list of five people who don't know Jesus so you could pray for them. Share with the group who you are praying for. Or, if you haven't done this yet, who could you be praying for?
6. Luke 2:19 says, "But Mary treasured up all these things and pondered them in her heart." What is one specific truth, encouragement, or challenge from God that you could "ponder" this week?

LUKE 3:1-20
7. Read Luke 3:1-20. In your own words, what was the message of John the Baptist?
8. John taught to three different kinds of people in the crowd: the soldiers who weren't content, the tax collectors who were cheating others, and the people with enough but who weren't sharing. Which of these do you struggle with the most (and why): generous sharing, cheating others, or contentment?

MATTHEW 4:13—4:17
9. What are some of the biggest temptations that you feel that you and your friends are facing?
10. What are some ways your Christian friends can help one another stand strong in the face of temptations?
11. Jesus was tempted just like we are. Why is this important? How does that make you feel?

BEFORE THE NEXT TIME:
In these readings, we've learned a lot of important truths about Jesus. Focus on one specific trait of Jesus and give thanks to God for sending his Son.

OVERVIEW

THE TEACHINGS OF JESUS

Jesus was a master teacher. He knew what his audience needed to hear and how to say it with authority. His message still rings true 2,000 years after his time on earth. This week, you are bound to be spiritually challenged and encouraged.

In your readings this week, you'll explore the Sermon on the Mount and several parables. This sermon holds some of Jesus' most famous teachings. As you read, take note of how often Jesus says, "You have heard... but I tell you..." Jesus was radical, and he taught that obedience begins in the heart. "Parable" literally means "to throw alongside." Jesus often used these "earthly stories" to communicate "heavenly truths." It's our responsibility to hear God's Word, love our neighbors, and have compassion for the lost.

These passages explore the following important questions:

- What kind of lifestyle does Jesus call me to?

- What does it look like to love others?

- What breaks God's heart?

56 THE SERMON ON THE MOUNT - PART 1

PRAY IT:
Jesus, thank You for Your teachings. I may not always want to hear them, but You always tell me what I need to know.

READ IT:
Matthew 5:1–6:4

THINK ABOUT IT:
Re-read Matthew 5:43-48. Revenge and retaliation are natural human responses: when we get hurt, we want to hurt back. Here's what's crazy: we never really feel better when we hurt others.

TRY IT:
Jesus was radical: he wants us to go against our natural urges. Is there someone who has caused you pain? What would it look like for you to refuse to strike back?

WRITE IT:
Before you finish, take a little time to write your thoughts, questions, concerns, and/or prayers here...

MEDITATE:

EPHESIANS 4:32
Be kind and compassionate to one another, forgiving each other, just as in Christ God forgave you.

57 THE SERMON ON THE MOUNT - PART 2

PRAY IT:
Father, thank You for caring for me. Help me not to worry about the problems I'm facing.

READ IT:
Matthew 6:5–7:29

THINK ABOUT IT:
Everyone struggles with anxiety and worry. What makes you worry the most? What do you typically do when you are worried? How does your worry keep you from putting God first?

TRY IT:
When you begin to worry this week, immediately say a quick prayer. Remind yourself that God knows the future, he provides everything you need, and he's bigger than any of your problems.

WRITE IT:
Before you finish, take a little time to write your thoughts, questions, concerns, and/or prayers here...

MEDITATE:

PSALM 37:4
Take delight in the Lord,
and he will give you the desires of your heart.

58 THE KINGDOM OF HEAVEN

PRAY IT:
Father, thank You for not leaving me alone. You are always with me, so help me to listen to Your Word.

READ IT:
Matthew 13

THINK ABOUT IT:
Jesus talked a lot about the Kingdom of God. Based on this parable, write a single sentence that explains a key characteristic of the Kingdom of God.

TRY IT:
Of the four soils, which one best describes your spiritual life right now? What do you need to do let God's Word bear fruit in your life?

WRITE IT:
Before you finish, take a little time to write your thoughts, questions, concerns, and/or prayers here...

MEDITATE:

JOHN 15:5-8
I am the vine; you are the branches. If you remain in me and I in you, you will bear much fruit; apart from me you can do nothing. If you do not remain in me, you are like a branch that is thrown away and withers; such branches are picked up, thrown into the fire and burned. If you remain in me and my words remain in you, ask whatever you wish, and it will be done for you. This is to my Father's glory, that you bear much fruit, showing yourselves to be my disciples.

THE TEACHINGS OF JESUS

59 THE GOOD SAMARITAN

PRAY IT:
Dear God, help me not to be too busy or too blind and miss opportunities to help people who are hurting.

READ IT:
Luke 10:25-37

THINK ABOUT IT:
Based on this passage, who are your "neighbors"? Be specific and write down their names. How are they hurting or in need? How does the following statement make you feel: "God wants to work through you to help others"?

TRY IT:
Pray for each person on your list by name. Ask God to help them and to create an opportunity for you to help them. When the moment comes this week, be brave and be faithful.

WRITE IT:
Before you finish, take a little time to write your thoughts, questions, concerns, and/or prayers here...

56-60

MEDITATE:

EPHESIANS 6:7
Serve wholeheartedly, as if you were serving the Lord, not people...

60 GOD LOVES THE LOST

PRAY IT:
Father, thank You for loving those who are lost. Help me to have a compassion like Yours.

READ IT:
Luke 15

THINK ABOUT IT:
What do these parables teach you about God? Is there anything surprising, encouraging, or confusing?

TRY IT:
Make a list of five people who are "lost"—who don't have a relationship with God. Make a commitment to pray for them regularly, serve them in practical ways, and speak up when the time is right. You might invite them to church, tell them you are a Christian, or ask them about their opinion of Jesus.

WRITE IT:
Before you finish, take a little time to write your thoughts, questions, concerns, and/or prayers here...

MEDITATE:

2 CORINTHIANS 5:16-21
So from now on we regard no one from a worldly point of view. Though we once regarded Christ in this way, we do so no longer. Therefore, if anyone is in Christ, the new creation has come: The old has gone, the new is here! All this is from God, who reconciled us to himself through Christ and gave us the ministry of reconciliation: that God was reconciling the world to himself in Christ, not counting people's sins against them. And he has committed to us the message of reconciliation. We are therefore Christ's ambassadors, as though God were making his appeal through us. We implore you on Christ's behalf: Be reconciled to God. God made him who had no sin to be sin for us, so that in him we might become the righteousness of God.

GROUP DISCUSSION QUESTIONS:

THE TEACHINGS OF JESUS

Purpose: To explore some of the major teachings of Jesus about living as one of his followers today.

MATTHEW 5:1-6:4

1. What would you say is the secret to true happiness? How can a person gain that happiness?
2. How would you describe Jesus' idea of true happiness given in the Sermon on the Mount? How does it compare with that of most people in our society?

MATTHEW 6:5-7:29

3. What do you suppose Jesus would say to a person sitting alone at lunch?
4. Which parts of the Sermon on the Mount are most encouraging, challenging, or confusing to you? Why?

MATTHEW 13

5. Jesus typically used parables to talk about the Kingdom of Heaven. How would you explain the Kingdom of Heaven to someone your age? How would you explain it to a person who doesn't go to church or follow Jesus?
6. What would it look like for you to be more sensitive to God's leading in your life? How could you have a regular connection with God's Word?

LUKE 10:25-37

7. When he was asked, "Who is my neighbor?" Jesus told the parable of the Good Samaritan. Based on his teaching, what are some of the biggest needs you see in others? How are the people you see every day hurting and in need?
8. What are some practical changes you could make to "love your neighbor" better this week?

LUKE 15

9. In the Parable of the Lost Son, who do you identify with the most: the younger brother, the father, or the older brother? Why?
10. What do you think is the main point Jesus is making through the three "Lost" parables in Luke 15?

BEFORE THE NEXT TIME:

During the next week, reflect on the things that you think, say, and do. Are you influenced more by the world or by Jesus' teachings? What would it look like for you to live more as a "citizen" of God's Kingdom in your everyday life?

OVERVIEW

THE MIRACLES OF JESUS

Jesus was God and his power is without limits. He healed the sick, fed thousands of people, cast out demons, controlled the weather, and defeated death. Jesus performed miracles to reveal his glory, to prove to the world that he was God. There is nothing that is beyond his power.

Jesus has the power to provide for our needs and he can conquer the storms we face. Jesus has power over the enemy, Satan, and he even has power over death itself. No other person in the Bible ever healed a blind man—Jesus is in a class by himself!

These passages explore the following important questions:

- Does Jesus care about my needs?
- Was Jesus really God?
- Does he have the power I need?

61 JESUS FEEDS MORE THAN 5,000 PEOPLE

PRAY IT:
God, thank You for providing for my needs.

READ IT:
Luke 9:1-36

THINK ABOUT IT:
In your opinion, why did Jesus do miracles? What purpose do they serve?

TRY IT:
Make a list of at least ten things God has provided for you. Look at the list three times today as a reminder to give thanks to God.

WRITE IT:
Before you finish, take a little time to write your thoughts, questions, concerns, and/or prayers here...

MEDITATE:

PSALM 9:1
I will give thanks to you, Lord, with all my heart;
I will tell of all your wonderful deeds.

62 JESUS WALKS ON WATER

PRAY IT:

Lord, I acknowledge Your awesome power. Thank You for looking after me.

READ IT:

Matthew 14:22-36

THINK ABOUT IT:

Jesus is the Son of God, and his power is greater than anything—even the storms. When the disciples were filled with fear, Jesus called them to have faith and trust in him.

TRY IT:

What are some of the "storms" in your life right now? What would it look like for you to have faith and get out of your "boat"? Practically speaking, how can you trust God with your problems?

WRITE IT:

Before you finish, take a little time to write your thoughts, questions, concerns, and/or prayers here...

MEDITATE:

PSALM 25:1-3

In you, Lord my God, I put my trust. I trust in you; do not let me be put to shame, nor let my enemies triumph over me. No one who hopes in you will ever be put to shame, but shame will come on those who are treacherous without cause.

63 JESUS HEALS A BLIND MAN

PRAY IT:
Jesus, open my eyes that I may see You more clearly and tell others about You.

READ IT:
John 9

THINK ABOUT IT:
The man born blind didn't have all the answers about Jesus. All he could do is share his story—"I was blind but now I see." None of the religious leaders could deny his story.

TRY IT:
What is your story? What could you share with others to help them understand how God has worked in your life? How were you "blind" and now you can "see"?

WRITE IT:
Before you finish, take a little time to write your thoughts, questions, concerns, and/or prayers here...

MEDITATE:

1 PETER 3:15
But in your hearts revere Christ as Lord. Always be prepared to give an answer to everyone who asks you to give the reason for the hope that you have. But do this with gentleness and respect...

64 JESUS HEALS A DEMON-POSSESSED MAN

PRAY IT:
Almighty God, thank You for my freedom. Without Your power I'd be alone to face my problems.

READ IT:
Mark 5:1-20

THINK ABOUT IT:
The man in this story was trapped by Satan. He was isolated and tormented, without friends or peace. Jesus healed him and gave him a mission to tell his world about God's mercy.

TRY IT:
Is there an area of your life where you need freedom? Submit this to God and share with a friend for prayer and support. Jesus sent this man home to "his people" so that he could share the good news with them. Who are the people in your life whom you can influence?

WRITE IT:
Before you finish, take a little time to write your thoughts, questions, concerns, and/or prayers here...

MEDITATE:

EPHESIANS 6:10-17
Finally, be strong in the Lord and in his mighty power. Put on the full armor of God, so that you can take your stand against the devil's schemes. For our struggle is not against flesh and blood, but against the rulers, against the authorities, against the powers of this dark world and against the spiritual forces of evil in the heavenly realms. Therefore put on the full armor of God, so that when the day of evil comes, you may be able to stand your ground, and after you have done everything, to stand. Stand firm then, with the belt of truth buckled around your waist, with the breastplate of righteousness in place, and with your feet fitted with the readiness that comes from the gospel of peace. In addition to all this, take up the shield of faith, with which you can extinguish all the flaming arrows of the evil one. Take the helmet of salvation and the sword of the Spirit, which is the word of God.

65 JESUS RAISES LAZARUS FROM THE DEAD

PRAY IT:

God, You are the creator. Thank You for another day of life. Help me to serve You faithfully.

READ IT:

John 11

THINK ABOUT IT:

Jesus has power over death. Not only did he raise Lazarus from the dead, he also defeated the death he experienced on the cross. God did both miracles so that we might believe in him.

TRY IT:

Is there an area in your life where you have a difficult time believing God? What would it look like for you to trust God?

WRITE IT:

Before you finish, take a little time to write your thoughts, questions, concerns, and/or prayers here...

MEDITATE:

JOHN 10:10

The thief comes only to steal and kill and destroy; I have come that they may have life, and have it to the full.

THE MIRACLES OF JESUS

GROUP DISCUSSION QUESTIONS:

THE MIRACLES OF JESUS

Purpose: To explore Jesus' miracles to uncover what they teach us about his power and authority.

LUKE 9:1-36

1. What do you believe about the miracles of Jesus? Did they really happen? Were they just tricks? Were they made up by the writers of the Bible? How does what you believe about the miracles impact your view of Jesus?
2. Do you believe that miracles still happen today? Why or why not? Have you seen any or heard about them happening?

MATTHEW 14:22-36

3. If Jesus were to calmly say to you, "Do not fear," what would be the one or two things you fear most?
4. Peter was bold! In spite of an uncontrollable storm raging around him, he still stepped out of the boat to meet Jesus. What was the last bold, risky thing you did because of your faith?

JOHN 9

5. In your opinion, why were the religious leaders skeptical about the blind man's healing? Would you have felt the same way? Why or why not?

6. Why do you think many people are skeptical about faith issues today? What is the best way to respond to a skeptic?

MARK 5:1-20

7. How does the media—movies, TV, etc.—portray evil? How does this conflict with what the Bible teaches?
8. The demon-possessed man was captive to a powerful force beyond his control. Where do you feel out of control in your life? What would it look like for you to stop trying to handle it on your own and give it over to Jesus?
9. What does this miracle—the healing of a demon-possessed man—teach you about Jesus?

JOHN 11

10. Jesus performed many miracles. Why do you think he did them? What is the purpose behind God's miracles?
11. How do you feel about your own death? What is your greatest source of hope for the future?

BEFORE THE NEXT TIME:

Jesus performed miracles to tell the world who he was and what he came to do. Before you begin the next set of readings, take some time to reflect on what you've learned about Jesus. What would it look like for you to trust God more next week?

OVERVIEW

THE CROSS

Jesus came to earth to give up his life as a ransom for the world. Without Jesus, we are captive to sin and death. Through faith in Jesus we have abundant life. Faith in Jesus means we believe that:

- Jesus actually suffered; it isn't just a story.

- Jesus literally died on the cross; it isn't a metaphor.

- Jesus genuinely defeated death; it isn't just a myth.

- Jesus really ascended into heaven; it isn't just an allegory.

In these passages, you'll get to see for yourself how these events unfolded as you explore Jesus' final weeks on earth.

These passages explore the following important questions:

- Does Jesus understand betrayal by a friend?

- Can I really believe who Jesus said he was?

- Is there any hope for me in this world?

66 THE LAST SUPPER

PRAY IT:

Jesus, thank You for Your love. Help me to remember You all day long.

READ IT:

Luke 22:1-46

THINK ABOUT IT:

The Jews celebrated Passover to remember their salvation from slavery in Egypt. Jesus died on the cross so humanity could have salvation from sin. (If you need a refresher on the Exodus, go back to day 20.)

TRY IT:

Why do you think Jesus said, in verse 19, "Do this in remembrance of me"? Do you think the disciples would forget? Do you ever forget about God and the things he's done for you?

WRITE IT:

Before you finish, take a little time to write your thoughts, questions, concerns, and/or prayers here...

MEDITATE:

1 CORINTHIANS 11:28

Everyone ought to examine themselves before they eat of the bread and drink from the cup.

67 JESUS IS ARRESTED

PRAY IT:
God, help me to live a life that honors You. I don't want to deny You in front of others with my words or my actions.

READ IT:
John 18

THINK ABOUT IT:
Peter walked with Jesus for three years. He knew all of Jesus' teachings and saw all of his miracles. Even in this, Peter still denied Jesus.

TRY IT:
In your life, where are you denying Jesus? God wants to be first place in our hearts; he wants all of our lives. The only way to give him everything is to give him the next thing. What is that next thing you will give him?

WRITE IT:
Before you finish, take a little time to write your thoughts, questions, concerns, and/or prayers here...

MEDITATE:

1 PETER 1:3-6
Praise be to the God and Father of our Lord Jesus Christ! In his great mercy he has given us new birth into a living hope through the resurrection of Jesus Christ from the dead, and into an inheritance that can never perish, spoil or fade. This inheritance is kept in heaven for you, who through faith are shielded by God's power until the coming of the salvation that is ready to be revealed in the last time. In all this you greatly rejoice, though now for a little while you may have had to suffer grief in all kinds of trials.

68 THE CRUCIFIXION

PRAY IT:
Powerful God, help me to endure the tough situations I'm facing. Even when I'm at the mercy of others, You are still in control.

READ IT:
John 19

THINK ABOUT IT:
As you read this passage, what feelings do you have? Is there anything shocking or surprising? When it comes to the crucifixion of Jesus, what is personally powerful for you?

TRY IT:
Jesus died for the sins of the world, taking our judgment so we wouldn't have to be punished. Take some time today to confess your sins to God and ask for forgiveness.

WRITE IT:
Before you finish, take a little time to write your thoughts, questions, concerns, and/or prayers here...

MEDITATE:

1 JOHN 1:9
If we confess our sins, he is faithful and just and will forgive us our sins and purify us from all unrighteousness.

69 THE RESURRECTION

PRAY IT:
Lord Jesus, thank You for defeating death so I can live with You for eternity. Help me to walk faithfully today.

READ IT:
John 20–21

THINK ABOUT IT:
Some people think the resurrection is just a myth, a made-up story. What do you think? Why does it matter? Thomas believed Jesus because he saw him with his own eyes. How have you seen God at work in your own life?

TRY IT:
Time to get honest: make a list of your deepest questions and doubts and begin praying for answers.

WRITE IT:
Before you finish, take a little time to write your thoughts, questions, concerns, and/or prayers here...

....

....

....

....

MEDITATE:

1 CORINTHIANS 15:12-14
But if it is preached that Christ has been raised from the dead, how can some of you say that there is no resurrection of the dead? If there is no resurrection of the dead, then not even Christ has been raised. And if Christ has not been raised, our preaching is useless and so is your faith.

70 THE ASCENSION

PRAY IT:
Thank You, God, that Jesus is alive in Heaven and has promised that he will return to earth someday.

READ IT:
Acts 1:1-11

THINK ABOUT IT:
Jesus lived a holy life, died for our sins, defeated death, and ascended into Heaven. God offers us the free gift of salvation through faith in Jesus. In your own words, what are your essential beliefs about Jesus?

TRY IT:
Jesus commissioned his disciples to be his witnesses to Jerusalem, Judea, and Samaria, and to the ends of the earth. What would it look like for you to be a witness to your world for Jesus?

WRITE IT:
Before you finish, take a little time to write your thoughts, questions, concerns, and/or prayers here...

....

....

....

MEDITATE:

MATTHEW 28:18-20
Then Jesus came to them and said, "All authority in heaven and on earth has been given to me. Therefore go and make disciples of all nations, baptizing them in the name of the Father and of the Son and of the Holy Spirit, and teaching them to obey everything I have commanded you. And surely I am with you always, to the very end of the age."

GROUP DISCUSSION QUESTIONS:

THE CROSS OF CHRIST

Purpose: To take a fresh look at the death and resurrection of Jesus and what that means for his followers today.

LUKE 22:1-46

1. Imagine you were at the Last Supper. What might you have felt and thought at this "First Communion"?
2. What helps you to remember Jesus? How could you be more intentional to remember what he has done for you? In your life, what are the biggest distractions that keep you from remembering him?

JOHN 18

3. How would you explain the motives, attitudes, and actions of Caiaphas, Pilate, and Peter during the arrest and trial of Jesus?
4. Pilate asked Jesus, "What is truth?" How would you answer this question? How does Jesus' answer shape your belief? Respond to this statement: "Many people ignore the truth in order to believe anything they want to preserve their comfort and keep living on their own terms."

JOHN 19

5. Why did so many people seem to hate Jesus? Do people still feel that way about him? What is so threatening about Jesus that people are against him?
6. For you personally, what is the significance of Jesus' death on the cross? Does his sacrifice have any impact on your day-to-day decisions or the problems you are facing?

JOHN 20-21

7. What is the most convincing evidence for you of the resurrection of Jesus?
8. Some people say that Jesus' resurrection is the "lynchpin" of the Christian faith. Do you agree or disagree? Why do you feel the way you do?

ACTS 1:1-11

9. Imagine that you had witnessed Jesus' ascension into Heaven. How do you think you would have felt? Explain.
10. In your opinion, what does it mean for you to be a witness for Jesus to your world?
11. At some point, Jesus will return to create a new heaven and earth. How can this hope for the future make an impact on your life today?

BEFORE THE NEXT TIME:
Think about what Jesus' death and resurrection means for the way you will live each moment of each day. What practical difference will it make? What happens in your life when you wander too far from this faith essential?

OVERVIEW

THE CHURCH IS BORN

The beginning of the Church was exciting: the disciples received the gift of the Holy Spirit, they preached boldly, they performed miracles, and many people came to faith in Jesus. They quickly faced opposition and they experienced trials and persecution. Stephen even gave up his life and was the first Christian martyr. Through the troubles, God was faithful. The disciples never lost hope, the Church grew, and many people came to know Jesus.

These passages explore the following important questions:

- Can I count on God for help to live a good life?

- What does it look like to stand up boldly for Jesus?

- Will I have to suffer for being a Christian? What will I have to give up?

71 THE HOLY SPIRIT

PRAY IT:
Father, thank You for empowering me to follow Your calling in my life. Help me to be bold wherever You are leading.

READ IT:
Acts 2

THINK ABOUT IT:
Pentecost is the Greek name for the Jewish festival "the Feast of Weeks" (Leviticus 23:15-22). This celebration happened 50 days after the Passover and the purpose was to thank God for the wheat harvest. What's the biggest thing you are thankful for today?

TRY IT:
How has God empowered you to do something bold in his name? If you were to speak to a large crowd like Peter did, what do you think you'd say?

WRITE IT:
Before you finish, take a little time to write your thoughts, questions, concerns, and/or prayers here...

MEDITATE:

1 CORINTHIANS 12:4-6
There are different kinds of gifts, but the same Spirit distributes them. There are different kinds of service, but the same Lord. There are different kinds of working, but in all of them and in everyone it is the same God at work.

72 GROWTH & PERSECUTION

PRAY IT:
Lord, help me to stand up for my faith, even when it's difficult and I fear rejection.

READ IT:
Acts 3–4

THINK ABOUT IT:
Have you ever had a conflict because of what you believe? What was the result? If not, how do you think you would act?

TRY IT:
Peter and John were "unschooled, ordinary men," but they had spent time with Jesus. How does it make you feel that God uses ordinary people to do great things? What does it look like for you to spend time with Jesus?

WRITE IT:
Before you finish, take a little time to write your thoughts, questions, concerns, and/or prayers here...

MEDITATE:

1 CORINTHIANS 16:13
Be on your guard; stand firm in the faith; be courageous; be strong.

73 STEPHEN DIES FOR HIS FAITH

PRAY IT:
God, give me an opportunity to tell someone about Your love, and help me to overcome my fears.

READ IT:
Acts 6:8–8:8

THINK ABOUT IT:
The people didn't like Stephen; they denied the truth and power of his message. In your opinion, why do some people in our world have a negative view of Christians?

TRY IT:
What would it look like for you to share your faith with a friend in a way that's clear, yet non-confrontational?

WRITE IT:
Before you finish, take a little time to write your thoughts, questions, concerns, and/or prayers here...

MEDITATE:

JOHN 15:20
Remember what I told you: "A servant is not greater than his master." If they persecuted me, they will persecute you also. If they obeyed my teaching, they will obey yours also.

74 PHILIP SHARES THE GOOD NEWS

PRAY IT:
Lord, thank You for the people who have helped me to understand You better. Help me to be a mentor to others.

READ IT:
Acts 8:26-40

THINK ABOUT IT:
Philip followed God's call and shared the good news about Jesus. Have you ever heard God tell you to do something? How did you know it was God? What did you do about it?

TRY IT:
If you were to have a spiritual conversation with someone who doesn't know Jesus, what would you say? Take a few moments and highlight the important things a person ought to know about Jesus.

WRITE IT:
Before you finish, take a little time to write your thoughts, questions, concerns, and/or prayers here...

MEDITATE:

ISAIAH 53:7-8
He was oppressed and afflicted, yet he did not open his mouth; he was led like a lamb to the slaughter, and as a sheep before its shearers is silent, so he did not open his mouth. By oppression and judgment he was taken away. Yet who of his generation protested? For he was cut off from the land of the living; for the transgression of my people he was punished.

75 GOOD NEWS FOR ALL

PRAY IT:
Jesus, thank You for loving the entire world. Help me to love everyone like You do.

READ IT:
Acts 10:1–11:18

THINK ABOUT IT:
Peter had some strong assumptions about the Kingdom of God; he didn't think it was for everyone. Be honest with yourself: is there anyone whom you think is "too bad" to be a follower of Jesus?

TRY IT:
Be more compassionate, understanding, and forgiving of others. What would it look like for you to build a bridge to those who are lost and don't yet have a relationship with God?

WRITE IT:
Before you finish, take a little time to write your thoughts, questions, concerns, and/or prayers here...

MEDITATE:

GALATIANS 3:28
There is neither Jew nor Gentile, neither slave nor free, nor is there male and female, for you are all one in Christ Jesus.

GROUP DISCUSSION QUESTIONS:

THE CHURCH IS BORN

Purpose: To examine the events surrounding the begining and growth of the early church and discover what they might mean for us today.

ACTS 2

1. What do you believe about the Holy Spirit? Does the Holy Spirit still "fill" people today? Why do you feel the way you do?
2. Have you ever sensed the Holy Spirit at work in your life? If so, how?

ACTS 3-4

3. What do you believe about the Church? What should it be like? What kind of community should it be? Name three things you love most about your church.
4. How can you give back to your church? What are two or three things you feel are missing from your church? What can you do to contribute to making these things happen?

ACTS 6:8-8:8

5. Stephen made the ultimate sacrifice for his faith—he gave up his life. What are some things you've had to give up because you are a follower of Jesus? What makes it so hard to let go?
6. Have you ever been ridiculed or persecuted for what you believe? If so, share what happened.

ACTS 8:26-40

7. The new church grew as people like Philip shared their faith. Have you ever shared your beliefs about God with another person? If so, what happened?
8. When it comes to being a witness for Jesus, it seems like there are two extremes. On one hand, Christians are very private about their faith and don't have many spiritual conversations. On the other, some believers are over-the-top vocal—maybe even obnoxious. Which way do you lean? How do you know when you are being too silent or too vocal?

ACTS 10:1-11:18

9. In your own words, define the gospel. How would you share the gospel with someone your own age?
10. It was difficult for Peter to accept Cornelius because his background and culture were so different. In what ways are you good at including others? What "kind" of people do you have a hard time including?

BEFORE THE NEXT TIME:
Set aside time soon to reflect on the significance of the coming of the Holy Spirit and the beginning of the early church. What can you learn from the community life of the Early Church? How did they deal with opposition and difficulties? Ask God to show you how you can make your church a better place.

OVERVIEW

THE TRAVELS OF PAUL

Paul traveled tirelessly all over the Roman Empire, preached the gospel fearlessly, and planted churches everywhere he went. God used Paul to write more than half of the New Testament. Paul was a true hero of the faith!

Before all of this, Paul hated Christians, even to the point of having them put to death.

The story of Paul is a tale of outrageous redemption. He literally saw the light and was knocked to the ground before he would listen to Jesus. After this life-changing encounter, Paul lived an incredible life of faith that is sure to challenge you to be a witness for Jesus in your world.

These passages explore the following important questions:

- Can God really use me to make a difference?
- What would it look like for everyone on my campus to hear about Jesus?
- What does it mean to be a witness for Jesus?

76 PAUL'S LIFE CHANGES

PRAY IT:

God, thank You for interrupting my life when I am on my own path. Help me to follow Your will for my life.

READ IT:

Acts 9:1-31

THINK ABOUT IT:

God used Saul, whose name was later changed to Paul, in spite of the fact that he persecuted Christians and even had them put to death. Do you ever let your past or your guilt keep you from doing great things for God?

TRY IT:

God interrupted Saul in a huge way: knocked him down and made him blind. How has God interrupted your life? Do you need an interruption now? How could you connect with God in a meaningful way today?

WRITE IT:

Before you finish, take a little time to write your thoughts, questions, concerns, and/or prayers here...

MEDITATE:

1 CORINTHIANS 15:9-11

For I am the least of the apostles and do not even deserve to be called an apostle, because I persecuted the church of God. But by the grace of God I am what I am, and his grace to me was not without effect. No, I worked harder than all of them—yet not I, but the grace of God that was with me. Whether, then, it is I or they, this is what we preach, and this is what you believed.

77 PAUL TELLS THE WORLD ABOUT JESUS

PRAY IT:
Dear God, thank You for having a plan for my life. Help me to understand my purpose so others can know You better.

READ IT:
Acts 13–14

THINK ABOUT IT:
After Paul got right with God, he traveled the world and told people about Jesus—even in the face of opposition and persecution! People believed in Jesus because of Paul's courageous faith. If you could do anything for Jesus, and you knew you wouldn't fail, what would you do?

TRY IT:
You may not have the same skills as Paul (and that's OK!), but what are some practical ways that you personally can make a difference for Jesus in your world?

WRITE IT:
Before you finish, take a little time to write your thoughts, questions, concerns, and/or prayers here...

MEDITATE:

MATTHEW 5:13-16

You are the salt of the earth. But if the salt loses its saltiness, how can it be made salty again? It is no longer good for anything, except to be thrown out and trampled underfoot. You are the light of the world. A town built on a hill cannot be hidden. Neither do people light a lamp and put it under a bowl. Instead they put it on its stand, and it gives light to everyone in the house. In the same way, let your light shine before others, that they may see your good deeds and glorify your Father in heaven.

78 THE COUNCIL AT JERUSALEM

PRAY IT:
God, thank You for the free gift of salvation. Help me to live a life of obedience.

READ IT:
Acts 15

THINK ABOUT IT:
This passage explores what it means to follow Jesus and be saved by him. Some people felt that following traditional customs was necessary for salvation. Paul and the disciples knew that we are saved by faith.

TRY IT:
In your opinion, what is the connection between faith and works (doing the right things)? We are saved by faith, so then why is doing the right thing important? How does this passage help you answer this question?

WRITE IT:
Before you finish, take a little time to write your thoughts, questions, concerns, and/or prayers here...

MEDITATE:

EPHESIANS 2:8-10
For it is by grace you have been saved, through faith—and this is not from yourselves, it is the gift of God—not by works, so that no one can boast. For we are God's handiwork, created in Christ Jesus to do good works, which God prepared in advance for us to do.

79 PAUL CONTINUES TO REACH THE WORLD

PRAY IT:
Dear God, even though I don't know the future, I trust You. Help me to have grace when I'm treated unfairly.

READ IT:
Acts 16–20

THINK ABOUT IT:
Paul and Silas were treated unfairly—not only were they falsely accused, but they also were beaten without a trial. When others treat you poorly, how do you typically respond? Does your response make others want to ask you about Jesus?

TRY IT:
In Acts 16:30, the jailer asked, "What must I do to be saved?" How would you answer this question if one of your friends asked you?

WRITE IT:
Before you finish, take a little time to write your thoughts, questions, concerns, and/or prayers here...

MEDITATE:

JOHN 3:16-17
For God so loved the world that he gave his one and only Son, that whoever believes in him shall not perish but have eternal life. For God did not send his Son into the world to condemn the world, but to save the world through him.

80 PAUL HEADS TO ROME

PRAY IT:
Lord, thank You for giving me eternal life. Open my heart so that I might know You more.

READ IT:
Acts 25–28

THINK ABOUT IT:
If you were on trial, accused of being a follower of Jesus, would there be enough evidence to "convict" you? Do the people who watch your life know that you are a Christian?

TRY IT:
In his defense, Paul offered up a "spiritual biography" of his life. Take some time today to create your own spiritual biography.

WRITE IT:
Before you finish, take a little time to write your thoughts, questions, concerns, and/or prayers here...

MEDITATE:

PHILIPPIANS 3:4-7
...though I myself have reasons for such confidence. If someone else thinks they have reasons to put confidence in the flesh, I have more: circumcised on the eighth day, of the people of Israel, of the tribe of Benjamin, a Hebrew of Hebrews; in regard to the law, a Pharisee; as for zeal, persecuting the church; as for righteousness based on the law, faultless. But whatever were gains to me I now consider loss for the sake of Christ.

GROUP DISCUSSION GUIDE:

THE TRAVELS OF PAUL

Purpose: To see how God can use unlikely people to spread the good news about Jesus and to consider how we can can make our mark in the world for Jesus.

ACTS 9:1-31

1. Paul had a dramatic experience of God on the road to Damascus. Why do you think God interrupted Paul's life like this? In what ways have you experienced divine interruptions?
2. Do you think it is possible to "see the light" about Jesus without having a dramatic experience like Paul's? Explain.

ACTS 13-14

3. Paul and Barnabas made a great team as they traveled and told people about Jesus. Do you have a friend or friends like this? What do you appreciate about them? What could you do to start a spiritual friendship like this with someone?
4. If you could do anything for Jesus and you knew you wouldn't fail, what would you do?

ACTS 15

5. The Council of Jerusalem settled a serious disagreement among early Christians. What does this passage teach you about how to resolve disagreements (with your family, friends, other believers)?
6. When you look at the root of many disagreements, you'll find unfair or un-communicated expectations. As you think about your last big disagreement, what was the root cause? Do you need to go back and apologize for something? What needs to be done to make things right?

ACTS 16-20

7. Paul traveled all across Asia sharing the gospel in spite of long distances or fierce opposition. Why do you think he was such a tenacious witness for Jesus?
8. Paul detoured from his intended destination to answer the call to go to Macedonia. Has God used a detour—done something unexpected—in your life to accomplish something good for you or others?

ACTS 25-28

9. On his way to Rome to face trial, how do you think Paul felt? Did he feel like things were out of control or going according to plan? Why do you feel the way you do?
10. Paul's purpose in life was to fulfill the call God gave him on the road to Damascus. What do you think God's call in your life is? What's your next step in fulfilling it?

BEFORE THE NEXT TIME:

The story of the spread of the gospel in Acts is unfinished. Every believer is called to play their part in fulfilling Acts 1:8—to be a witness for Jesus. Spend time in the week ahead asking God to reveal his purpose for your life and ask for specific next steps you can take.

OVERVIEW

PAUL'S LETTERS TO THE CHURCHES

Typically, Paul didn't stay in one place for very long. In order to encourage and equip local churches, he often wrote them letters. These letters were intended to be read publicly and shared with the surrounding churches.

While each church had different needs, Paul wanted to be sure that every church remained focused on Christ. Through Jesus, every believer has the power to fight sin and temptation. Paul also paints a vivid picture for living a life that is pleasing to God. While there is an unseen, yet real, enemy in the world, we have protection against the devil. No matter what situation we are facing, joy is always an option in Christ. Above everything, Jesus is supreme in power and glory.

These passages explore the following important questions:

- Where can I find the power not to sin?
- What should my life look like if I follow the Holy Spirit?
- Is Jesus really the answer?

81 MORE THAN CONQUERORS

PRAY IT:
Father, I am thankful that there is nothing I will face today that is bigger than You.

READ IT:
Romans 8

THINK ABOUT IT:
If God is for us, who can be against us? When you face a difficult problem, person, or situation, what makes it difficult to trust in God's power?

TRY IT:
Think of someone you know who is facing some big issues. Commit to praying for them every day this week and follow God's leading if there's a way you can help.

WRITE IT:
Before you finish, take a little time to write your thoughts, questions, concerns, and/or prayers here...

MEDITATE:

ISAIAH 41:10
So do not fear, for I am with you; do not be dismayed, for I am your God. I will strengthen you and help you; I will uphold you with my righteous right hand.

82. THE FRUIT OF THE SPIRIT

PRAY IT:

God, thank You for giving my life purpose and meaning. Help me to bear fruit according to Your will.

READ IT:

Galatians 5:16–6:10

THINK ABOUT IT:

This passage contrasts the spiritual life with a life of sin. What habits, desires, or attitudes make you a slave to sin?

TRY IT:

Paul urges us to watch our lives so that we may not be tempted and fall into sin. Practically speaking, what does this look like for you personally?

WRITE IT:

Before you finish, take a little time to write your thoughts, questions, concerns, and/or prayers here...

MEDITATE:

MATTHEW 7:15-20

Watch out for false prophets. They come to you in sheep's clothing, but inwardly they are ferocious wolves. By their fruit you will recognize them. Do people pick grapes from thorn bushes, or figs from thistles? Likewise, every good tree bears good fruit, but a bad tree bears bad fruit. A good tree cannot bear bad fruit, and a bad tree cannot bear good fruit. Every tree that does not bear good fruit is cut down and thrown into the fire. Thus, by their fruit you will recognize them.

83 THE ARMOR OF GOD

PRAY IT:
God, protect me from the dangers I face, both the seen and the unseen.

READ IT:
Ephesians 6:10-20

THINK ABOUT IT:
Do you think spiritual warfare is real? Is it just superstition? Have you ever experienced it?

TRY IT:
Go personal and practical. Consider what the armor of God ought to look like in your life: truth, righteousness, ready to share the gospel, faith, salvation, the Word of God.

WRITE IT:
Before you finish, take a little time to write your thoughts, questions, concerns, and/or prayers here...

MEDITATE:

HEBREWS 4:12
For the word of God is alive and active. Sharper than any double-edged sword, it penetrates even to dividing soul and spirit, joints and marrow; it judges the thoughts and attitudes of the heart.

84 REJOICE IN THE LORD

PRAY IT:
Father, You have given me so much to be thankful for. Help me to remember Your blessings all day long.

READ IT:
Philippians 4:4-9

THINK ABOUT IT:
Happiness is based on external circumstances. When our situation is good, we're happy. When it's bad, the happiness goes away. Joy is based on the eternal promises of God. Do you live more out of happiness or joy?

TRY IT:
Make a list of 20 things you are thankful for and express your gratitude to God.

WRITE IT:
Before you finish, take a little time to write your thoughts, questions, concerns, and/or prayers here...

MEDITATE:

1 THESSALONIANS 5:16-17
Rejoice always, pray continually.

85 THE SUPREMACY OF CHRIST

PRAY IT:
Jesus, there is no one like You. Help me to glorify Your name and to trust in Your power before trusting in anything else.

READ IT:
Colossians 1:1-23

THINK ABOUT IT:
What is surprising, inspiring, or confusing in this passage? What do you learn about Jesus?

TRY IT:
Make a list and think about the biggest things you've seen, the most awesome forces in our world, and the powerful stuff that shapes your life. Now imagine that Jesus is bigger than all these things. How might this wonder impact your life?

WRITE IT:
Before you finish, take a little time to write your thoughts, questions, concerns, and/or prayers here...

MEDITATE:

JOHN 1:3
Through him all things were made; without him nothing was made that has been made.

GROUP DISCUSSION QUESTIONS:

PAUL'S LETTERS TO THE CHURCHES

Purpose: To explore what it means to be a godly leader, to handle money well, to pursue holiness, and to make God's Word a foundation in our lives.

ROMANS 8

1. Would you say anything "controls" you? What seems to influence most of your decisions?
2. In your opinion, what do you think it means to be "controlled by the Spirit"? Does the Holy Spirit influence your life? How could you become more "controlled" by the Spirit?

GALATIANS 5:16–6:10

3. As you read through the "fruit of the Spirit," which two or three seem to come easiest for you? How do you see these qualities impact your relationships?
4. Which one of the "fruits" poses the greatest challenge for you? What makes it a difficult struggle? What kinds of situations really put you to the test in this area?

EPHESIANS 6:10-20

5. How often do you think about spiritual warfare as a reality in your life? Some people fall to one extreme or the other: either seeing everything as spiritual warfare or ignoring it altogether. What would it look like for you to have a healthy balance?
6. Realistically speaking, what should your prayer life look like? How often should you pray? What should you be praying for? What reminders can you place in your life to keep you focused and talking to God on a regular basis?

PHILIPPIANS 4:4-9

7. Paul tells the Philippian church to "rejoice in the Lord always." Is that really possible? Why do you think the way you do? When is it easy for you to rejoice? When are you most tested?
8. In your own words, what's the difference between happiness and joy? Why do we often settle for less than joy, for mere happiness, when we can have so much more?

COLOSSIANS 1:1-23

9. Based on this passage, how does Paul describe Jesus?
10. Respond to this statement: "If you act like a Christian, you are a Christian, whether you believe in Jesus Christ or not."

BEFORE THE NEXT TIME:
Make a list of what you have learned about Jesus in these readings. Then, take time to thank him for who he is and for what he has done for you in his death and resurrection. Learn to rejoice, no matter how difficult things may get.

OVERVIEW

PAUL'S LETTERS TO THE LEADERS

Timothy was one of Paul's disciples and a leader in the church. They were close, as Paul calls Timothy his "son in the faith." In his letters to Timothy, Paul covers a wide range of topics so that everyone would know how they "ought to conduct themselves in God's household" (1 Timothy 3:14).

In your readings this week, you will explore God's standard for church leaders, the dangers of loving money, the importance of pursing righteousness, how to deal with false teachers, and the purpose of Scripture. The passage in the final devotional is written to the Thessalonians, and it includes instructions about the Day of the Lord.

These passages explore the following important questions:

- What does it look like to be a leader in God's family?

- What place should money have in my life?

- Why is Scripture important for me?

86 ELDERS & DEACONS

PRAY IT:
Lord, thank You for the pastors and other spiritual leaders You have put in my life.

READ IT:
1 Timothy 3

THINK ABOUT IT:
Using your own words, rephrase the leadership characteristics from this passage. In your opinion, why are such high standards important?

TRY IT:
Pray for each of your church leaders every day this week. Of the leader qualities in this passage, which one do you have the most difficulty with? Why?

WRITE IT:
Before you finish, take a little time to write your thoughts, questions, concerns, and/or prayers here...

MEDITATE:

MATTHEW 20:24-28
When the ten heard about this, they were indignant with the two brothers. Jesus called them together and said, "You know that the rulers of the Gentiles lord it over them, and their high officials exercise authority over them. Not so with you. Instead, whoever wants to become great among you must be your servant, and whoever wants to be first must be your slave—just as the Son of Man did not come to be served, but to serve, and to give his life as a ransom for many."

87 THE LOVE OF MONEY

PRAY IT:
Lord, thank You for the material blessings I have in my life. Keep me from greed and bless me with contentment.

READ IT:
1 Timothy 6:3-21

THINK ABOUT IT:
What does this passage teach about the dangers of money? Have you experienced any of these pitfalls?

TRY IT:
What would it look like for you to practice "godliness with contentment"?

WRITE IT:
Before you finish, take a little time to write your thoughts, questions, concerns, and/or prayers here...

MEDITATE:

HEBREWS 13:5-6
Keep your lives free from the love of money and be content with what you have, because God has said, "Never will I leave you; never will I forsake you." So we say with confidence, "The Lord is my helper; I will not be afraid. What can mere mortals do to me?"

88 TEMPTATION & GRACE

PRAY IT:
Dear God, give me the strength to face temptation. Help me to rely on Your grace when I stumble.

READ IT:
2 Timothy 2

THINK ABOUT IT:
2 Timothy 2:14 says, "Flee the evil desires of youth." Based on what you see in your life and the struggles of your friends, what do you think are the main temptations students are facing?

TRY IT:
2 Timothy 2:1 says, "Be strong in the grace that is in Christ Jesus." What does it look like for you personally to walk in God's grace? How can you experience it every day?

WRITE IT:
Before you finish, take a little time to write your thoughts, questions, concerns, and/or prayers here...

MEDITATE:

HEBREWS 4:16
Let us then approach God's throne of grace with confidence, so that we may receive mercy and find grace to help us in our time of need.

89 ALL SCRIPTURE IS GOD-BREATHED

PRAY IT:
Jesus, help me to love Your Word more and more. Help me to trust Your truth more than my own feelings.

READ IT:
2 Timothy 3:10–4:8

THINK ABOUT IT:
The Bible isn't just another book, it's God's love letter, written to us to draw us closer to him. Do you believe the Bible is true? What role does the Bible play in your life?

TRY IT:
Near the end of his life, Paul said, "I have fought the good fight, I have finished the race, I have kept the faith." What would it take for you to be able to graduate from high school without graduating from your faith? What commitments can you make today to set yourself up to "finish the race"?

WRITE IT:
Before you finish, take a little time to write your thoughts, questions, concerns, and/or prayers here...

MEDITATE:

HEBREWS 4:12
For the word of God is alive and active. Sharper than any double-edged sword, it penetrates even to dividing soul and spirit, joints and marrow; it judges the thoughts and attitudes of the heart.

90 THE RETURN OF THE KING

PRAY IT:

Father, thank You for holding the universe in Your hands. I have no idea what the future holds, but I know You do and that You love me.

READ IT:

1 Thessalonians 4:13–5:11

THINK ABOUT IT:

One day, Jesus will return to earth. All who believe in him will spend eternity in perfect relationship with God. How could having an unshakable hope for the future impact your life today?

TRY IT:

In light of the hope of Heaven, Paul teaches us to encourage and build one another up. Who could you encourage today? Could you go beyond kind words and offer spiritual encouragement?

WRITE IT:

Before you finish, take a little time to write your thoughts, questions, concerns, and/or prayers here...

MEDITATE:

REVELATION 21:1-5

Then I saw "a new heaven and a new earth," for the first heaven and the first earth had passed away, and there was no longer any sea. I saw the Holy City, the new Jerusalem, coming down out of heaven from God, prepared as a bride beautifully dressed for her husband. And I heard a loud voice from the throne saying, "Look! God's dwelling place is now among the people, and he will dwell with them. They will be his people, and God himself will be with them and be their God. 'He will wipe every tear from their eyes. There will be no more death' or mourning or crying or pain, for the old order of things has passed away." He who was seated on the throne said, "I am making everything new!" Then he said, "Write this down, for these words are trustworthy and true."

GROUP DISCUSSION QUESTIONS:

PAUL LETTERS TO THE LEADERS

Purpose: To learn more about the qualifications for leadership in the church, how to live a godly life, and the fundamental importance of the Bible.

1 TIMOTHY 3

1. Which leadership characteristics given by Paul in this passage are most common in Christian leaders you know? Which ones seem to be most uncommon?
2. It's clear that Jesus' leadership is different from the way the world leads. In your own words, what are the differences? How should Christian leaders be different from worldly leaders?

1 TIMOTHY 6:3-21

3. Based on this passage, how would you summarize Paul's teaching about money? Where does this teaching challenge you personally?
4. Think about our world's view of money: what does the world "teach" about money? How does the pursuit of more money and more stuff have a negative impact on relationships?

2 TIMOTHY 2

5. What do Paul's images of a soldier, athlete, and farmer teach you about being a follower of Jesus Christ?
6. What are some things that tend to distract you from doing the things God wants you to do? How can you avoid these distractions?

2 TIMOTHY 3:10-4:8

7. Paul says that those who want to live a godly life will be persecuted. What does this mean? Have you ever been treated unfairly because of your beliefs?
8. Everyone has a foundation for truth. Typically, the average person's values come from their personal feelings and selfish desires. What could it look like for you to let God's Word be the ultimate authority for your life?

1 THESSALONIANS 4:13-5:11

9. What do you think it means to be "alert" for Christ's return? What should it look like for you to be ready? How can this readiness impact your day-to-day decisions?
10. It's impossible to live without hope. Everyone is looking forward to something in the future—even if it's just to "get through another day." What are the things you hope in the most? What would it look like for you to add more spiritual hope to your life?

BEFORE THE NEXT TIME:
Paul urges Timothy to be a faithful teacher of God's Word, and to set a godly example in speech, conduct, love, faith, and purity. He urges everyone to be alert and ready for Christ's return. Spend time this week asking God to show you how you can cultivate these qualities in your life more deeply.

OVERVIEW

THE APOSTLES' TEACHING

These readings focus on teachings from James, Peter, John, and Paul. These apostles were all inspired by the Holy Spirit, yet each one has a unique perspective that adds to our understanding of what it means to live a Christian life. Over the next five days, you'll be challenged to pursue a deeper understanding of love, what it means to be made new, pursuing holiness, and the connection between faith and works.

These passages explore the following important questions:

- What does it really mean to love others?

- Can I be sure that I'm fully free from my past?

- Since God forgives, why can't I just keep living selfishly and ask for forgiveness when I need it?

91 THE MOST EXCELLENT WAY

PRAY IT:
Father, thank You for loving me unconditionally. Teach me to reflect Your love to the world.

READ IT:
1 Corinthians 13

THINK ABOUT IT:
In your own words, describe the essence of what it means to love others. In the list that Paul gives us, which aspects are most challenging for you? Which ones are most meaningful?

TRY IT:
Take a quick inventory of your relationships (friends, family, etc.). Are there two or three that ought to be deepened? How could you express love to them today or this week?

WRITE IT:
Before you finish, take a little time to write your thoughts, questions, concerns, and/or prayers here...

MEDITATE:

ROMANS 13:8
Let no debt remain outstanding, except the continuing debt to love one another, for whoever loves others has fulfilled the law.

92 A NEW CREATION IN CHRIST

PRAY IT:
Lord, You make all things new! Thank You for renewing my heart and making me more like You.

READ IT:
2 Corinthians 4:1–6:2

THINK ABOUT IT:
In what ways has God made you a new creation? What does it mean that the old is gone? Is there anything in your past that you are glad to leave behind?

TRY IT:
An ambassador is authorized to represent another person who isn't present. Our president can't be in every country, so he sends ambassadors as representatives. What could it look like for you to be an ambassador for Christ on your campus this week?

WRITE IT:
Before you finish, take a little time to write your thoughts, questions, concerns, and/or prayers here...

MEDITATE:

LAMENTATIONS 3:22-24
Because of the Lord's great love we are not consumed, for his compassions never fail. They are new every morning; great is your faithfulness. I say to myself, "The Lord is my portion; therefore I will wait for him."

93 THE PURSUIT OF HOLINESS

PRAY IT:
Almighty Lord, You are the God of the universe and there is no one like You. Help me to become more like You.

READ IT:
1 Peter 1:1–2:12

THINK ABOUT IT:
"Holy" literally means separate or unique. It is one of God's primary characteristics because he is completely different from all of creation. As you consider God's holiness, what images comes to mind? How does God's holiness make you feel?

TRY IT:
God calls us to be holy like he is holy. Why do you think God wants this for us? Based on this passage, what is one change you can make to be more holy?

WRITE IT:
Before you finish, take a little time to write your thoughts, questions, concerns, and/or prayers here…

....

....

....

MEDITATE:

PSALM 28:2-9
Hear my cry for mercy as I call to you for help, as I lift up my hands toward your Most Holy Place. Do not drag me away with the wicked, with those who do evil, who speak cordially with their neighbors but harbor malice in their hearts. Repay them for their deeds and for their evil work; repay them for what their hands have done and bring back on them what they deserve. Because they have no regard for the deeds of the Lord and what his hands have done, he will tear them down and never build them up again. Praise be to the Lord, for he has heard my cry for mercy. The Lord is my strength and my shield; my heart trusts in him, and he helps me. My heart leaps for joy, and with my song I praise him. The Lord is the strength of his people, a fortress of salvation for his anointed one. Save your people and bless your inheritance; be their shepherd and carry them forever.

THE APOSTLES' TEACHING

94 FAITH & WORKS

PRAY IT:
Father, help me to do good things in Your name. Thank You for loving me unconditionally and saving me by grace through faith in Your son, Jesus.

READ IT:
James 1–2

THINK ABOUT IT:
We're not saved by what we do; it is through Jesus' work that we are saved by faith. Faith comes first; obedience (deeds) comes second. Why is it dangerous when we switch the order?

TRY IT:
James is clear: faith without deeds is dead. How well have you been expressing your faith in the past two weeks? Is there an area where you need to "step up" your obedience?

WRITE IT:
Before you finish, take a little time to write your thoughts, questions, concerns, and/or prayers here...

MEDITATE:

ROMANS 10:10
For it is with your heart that you believe and are justified, and it is with your mouth that you profess your faith and are saved.

95 LOVING ONE ANOTHER

PRAY IT:
Father, thank You for loving me unconditionally. There is nothing I can do to make You stop loving me. Forgive me for the times I get caught up trying to earn Your approval.

READ IT:
1 John 3:11–4:21

THINK ABOUT IT:
Love is all about sacrifice. What's the greatest expression of love that you have ever experienced? How did it make you feel?

TRY IT:
Jesus gave up his life because he loves us. What would it look like for you to love sacrificially this week? What do you need to give up so you can love others more like Jesus?

WRITE IT:
Before you finish, take a little time to write your thoughts, questions, concerns, and/or prayers here...

MEDITATE:

JOHN 10:11
I am the good shepherd. The good shepherd lays down his life for the sheep.

GROUP DISCUSSION GUIDE:

THE APOSTLES' TEACHING

Purpose: To explore in greater depth more of what it means to live a life that pleases God and reflects his Spirit working within us.

1 CORINTHIANS 13

1. 1 Corinthians 13 is often called "the love chapter" because it describes the essence of real love. What's the greatest example of love you've seen or experienced?
2. Why do you think that Paul says love is the greatest virtue? Why did he choose love and not something else?

2 CORINTHIANS 4:1–6:2

3. Paul says, "We have renounced secret and shameful ways" (4:2). What are some old habits or lifestyle choices that you've given up (or need to give up) since Jesus has made you a new creation?
4. Although we are made new in Christ, we still make mistakes and live contrary to God's design for our lives. When you sin, what do you think God wants us to do?
5. In your own words, what is the ministry of reconciliation? What are some practical ways you can share this message with your friends?

1 PETER 1:1–2:12

6. Since Jesus defeated death and offers us salvation through faith, we have "an inheritance that can never perish, spoil or fade." What does this mean for you? How does it add perspective to your life?
7. Peter urges us to "love one another deeply, from the heart." How is this different from the kind of love we see in our world: people we know, the songs we listen to, and the shows we watch?

JAMES 1–2

8. Consider some of the biggest trials you have faced. How did they make you a better person? What did you learn? How did God help you through these times?
9. What do you think is the proper relationship between faith and works (good deeds)? Is one more important than the other? If we only need to believe to gain salvation, because it's a gift and not something we earn from good deeds, then why are works important?

1 JOHN 3:11–4:21

10. In your opinion, what are the characteristics of a true Christian? How does this compare with this passage?
11. Jesus sacrificed his life for the world so that we might know him and be in his family. Practically speaking, what does it look like for you to "lay down" your life for the people you know?

BEFORE THE NEXT TIME:

Set aside time this week to reflect on these passages and what you have learned. Ask God to help you love with his love so that you can be an effective ambassador for him. Bring to God any trials you face and pray that you will grow through them.

OVERVIEW

REVELATION

These readings bring us to the end of the Bible and the end of E100®. "In the beginning" (Genesis 1:1) God created everything from nothing, and in the end, Jesus promises to make all things new (Revelation 21:5).

Revelation (not "revelations") was written by the Apostle John. He had now grown old and was living in exile on an island because of his faith in Jesus. He knew what it meant to follow Jesus and live a life of love.

This large letter tells the story of the end of the world, quite literally, the apocalypse. The imagery and word pictures are awe-inspiring. The only thing more magnificent and fantastic is the message of Revelation, which is, in short: God is in control and he "wins" in the end. Actually, there's not even a contest between good and evil. There is no struggle. Evil simply loses.

Our response is to live faithfully and wait for Jesus to return.

These passages explore the following important questions:

- What will happen at the end of the world?

- Is God really still involved and at work in the world?

- How can I live today, in light of what's happening at the end of time?

96 A VOICE & A VISION

PRAY IT:
Thank You, Lord God, for speaking to me. Help me to hear You clearly so that I may become more like You.

READ IT:
Revelation 1

THINK ABOUT IT:
Based on this passage, and everything you remember from your E100® journey, make a list of who Jesus is and what he means to you.

TRY IT:
The Apostle John experienced an incredible vision of Jesus. What can you do to be more open to hearing God's voice in your life? How can you make reading the Bible, on your own, become a regular habit?

WRITE IT:
Before you finish, take a little time to write your thoughts, questions, concerns, and/or prayers here...

MEDITATE:

ISAIAH 44:6
This is what the Lord says—Israel's King and Redeemer, the Lord Almighty: "I am the first and I am the last; apart from me there is no God."

97 MESSAGES TO THE CHURCHES

PRAY IT:
Father, Your Word holds both encouragements and warnings. Help me to listen carefully to both.

READ IT:
Revelation 2–3

THINK ABOUT IT:
Consider the messages to each of the seven churches. Which one do you identify with the most? Which one did you need to hear today? Why?

TRY IT:
In these chapters, several times Jesus urges the Church to repent. Repentance is a change of mind and purpose. In your life, where do you need to repent to God? What does this surrender look like for you personally?

WRITE IT:
Before you finish, take a little time to write your thoughts, questions, concerns, and/or prayers here...

MEDITATE:

DEUTERONOMY 30:11-15
Now what I am commanding you today is not too difficult for you or beyond your reach. It is not up in heaven, so that you have to ask, "Who will ascend into heaven to get it and proclaim it to us so we may obey it?" Nor is it beyond the sea, so that you have to ask, "Who will cross the sea to get it and proclaim it to us so we may obey it?" No, the word is very near you; it is in your mouth and in your heart so you may obey it. See, I set before you today life and prosperity, death and destruction.

98 THE THRONE OF HEAVEN

PRAY IT:
God in Heaven, You alone are worthy to be worshipped. You have created the universe and everything in it.

READ IT:
Revelation 4–7

THINK ABOUT IT:
What picture of heaven do you get as you read these verses? How does it make you feel? Since God is the creator of everything, why do we sometimes worship other things?

TRY IT:
Re-read Revelation 4:11 out loud and make it your prayer. Write it out word-for-word in the space below. Today, keep a close watch for the times that you treat something other than God as more worthy of your attention and praise.

WRITE IT:
Before you finish, take a little time to write your thoughts, questions, concerns, and/or prayers here...

MEDITATE:

ISAIAH 6:1-6
In the year that King Uzziah died, I saw the Lord, high and exalted, seated on a throne; and the train of his robe filled the temple. Above him were seraphim, each with six wings: With two wings they covered their faces, with two they covered their feet, and with two they were flying. And they were calling to one another: "Holy, holy, holy is the Lord Almighty; the whole earth is full of his glory." At the sound of their voices the doorposts and thresholds shook and the temple was filled with smoke. "Woe to me!" I cried. "I am ruined! For I am a man of unclean lips, and I live among a people of unclean lips, and my eyes have seen the King, the Lord Almighty." Then one of the seraphim flew to me with a live coal in his hand, which he had taken with tongs from the altar.

99 HALLELUJAH!

PRAY IT:
God, thank You for Your constant care and presence in my life. I praise Your name with all my soul!

READ IT:
Revelation 19–20

THINK ABOUT IT:
Hallelujah is a Hebrew word that means "praise the Lord." In these chapters, why is God being praised?

TRY IT:
Write out your own song or prayer that praises God for his salvation, blessings, and power at work in your life. Make it as personal as possible!

WRITE IT:
Before you finish, take a little time to write your thoughts, questions, concerns, and/or prayers here...

MEDITATE:

PSALM 104:1
Praise the Lord, my soul.
Lord my God, you are very great;
you are clothed with splendor and majesty.

100 THE NEW JERUSALEM

PRAY IT:
Father, thank You for drawing me closer to You. Help me to keep my hope focused on You.

READ IT:
Revelation 21–22

THINK ABOUT IT:
In the end, all things will be made new. As you imagine Heaven, how have these chapters shaped your picture of eternity with God? What is shocking or surprising from this Scripture?

TRY IT:
Anytime you turn on a light today, think of Jesus as the light of the world now, and when the heavens and the earth are made new.

WRITE IT:
Before you finish, take a little time to write your thoughts, questions, concerns, and/or prayers here...

MEDITATE:

ROMANS 5:1-2
Therefore, since we have been justified through faith, we have peace with God through our Lord Jesus Christ, through whom we have gained access by faith into this grace in which we now stand. And we boast in the hope of the glory of God.

GROUP DISCUSSION QUESTIONS:

REVELATION

Purpose: To understand what will happen at the end of this age, and to see how Christ and his followers continue to be an integral part of God's plan for the world.

REVELATION 1

1. What do you learn about Jesus in the first chapter of Revelation? Does any of it surprise, inspire, or confuse you? Explain.
2. Jesus told John not to be afraid. Why did Jesus need to say this? What is a fear in your life that you can give to God? Is there anything about God that makes you afraid? If so, what is it?

REVELATION 2-3

3. After reading John's letters to the seven churches, how do you think Jesus would feel about your life and how you live in community with others?
4. In your own words, what is your view of heaven? What is it like and who is it for?

REVELATION 4-7

5. What if God asked you, "Why should I let you into heaven?" What would you say? Are you confident you'd get in? Why or why not? Do you think God wants us to be sure or to live in uncertainty?
6. The later chapters of Revelation speak of the final judgment and the return of Jesus Christ. Why is it important that we know about these things? How can this knowledge impact your daily life?

REVELATION 19-20

7. Satan is real, he's not a myth, and he's actively at work against God's plan. In the end, it's clear that he is defeated. How does this make you feel? How can this strengthen your daily struggles against temptation?
8. At the end of time, everyone will be held accountable for the things we believed and the choices we made. Why is it important for you personally to keep this in mind?

REVELATION 21-22

9. Re-read Revelation 21:1-5. What are you looking forward to the most once we enter the new heavens and new earth?
10. Our ultimate purpose is to worship God—to focus on him first, as the most important priority in our lives. When is it easiest for you to worship God? What are the big distractions in your life that keep you from being focused on him?

CONGRATULATIONS!
WAY TO GO!
YOU'VE COMPLETED THE E100!

You have prayed, read, and reflected on 100 essential passages from the Bible. That's a huge accomplishment, and you should celebrate—Really! It's a big deal and few are disciplined enough to complete the whole thing. We hope you share the good news with someone close to you.

But, the journey isn't over. We want to encourage you to keep growing in your faith, drawing closer to God and becoming more like him. Continue to meet God daily in prayer, reading the Bible, and reflecting on its meaning for your life.

We have created another study much like this one called *The Essential Jesus*. Now that you have an overview of the Bible and God's great story of redemption, dig deeper into Jesus. In *The Essential Jesus* journey, you'll explore 100 of the most important passages about Jesus. Everywhere that Jesus went, he drew a crowd and people were amazed. We think you will be too. Try to think of one friend you can invite to journey with you as you discover more about our Savior, God's Son, Jesus.

AUTHOR BIOS

DOUG FIELDS

Doug Fields has a long history of youth ministry influence. First and foremost he has been a youth pastor for over 30 years at both Mariners and Saddleback Church in Southern California. He has been a speaker and trainer for Youth Specialties for 25 years, he founded Simply Youth Ministry (now owned by Group Publishing), and he is the co-founder of DownloadYouthMinistry.com. A prolific author and co-author of over 60 books, Doug is thrilled to partner with Scripture Union and be part of the Essential Jesus and Essential 100 products. You can find more about Doug, his family, his books, and his ministry at www.dougfields.com.

MATT McGILL

Matt McGill is a veteran youth worker who has a passion to help students draw closer to Jesus. Many of his spiritual growth tools, resources, and sermons can be found on www.DownloadYouthMinistry.com which Matt co-founded. He is married and has five kids—all of whom are boys. In spite of many hours of practice, he is still a below-average gamer.

WHITNEY T. KUNIHOLM

Whitney T. Kuniholm is the President of Scripture Union USA (ScriptureUnion.org), author of several books including *The Essential 100*, *The Essential Jesus*, and *The Essential Question*, and is a frequent contributor to Scripture Union's quarterly Bible reading guide, *Encounter with God*. He also has a blog (EssentialBibleBlog.com) and speaks at churches and Christian conferences.

NOTES

NOTES

NOTES